THE MANAGER'S POCKET GUIDE TO
Using Consultants

David Newman

HRD PRESS, INC.
Amherst, Massachusetts

Copyright © 2014, HRD Press, Inc.

All rights reserved. No part of this publication may be reproduced or transmitted in any form or by any means, electronic or mechanical, including photocopy, recording, or used in an information storage or retrieval system, without prior written permission from the author.

Published by: HRD Press, Inc.
 22 Amherst Road
 1-800-822-2801
 (U.S. and Canada)
 1-413-253-3488
 1-413-253-3490 (Fax)
 www.hrdpress.com

ISBN 0-87425-923-1

Cover design by Eileen Klockars
Production services by Anctil Virtual Office
Editorial services by Suzanne Bay and Sally Farnham

Table of Contents

Introduction	1
Chapter 1: A Field Guide to Consultants	**3**
Consultants: Who They Are	4
What Consultants Do	4
The Roles Consultants Play	5
Alternatives to Using Consultants	7
When to Bring in a Consultant (and When *Not* To)	8
Reasons to Use a Consultant	10
Key Questions to Ask a Prospective Consultant	10
Chapter 2: Establishing the Relationship	**13**
Preparing for the Consulting Project	13
Establishing Roles and Responsibilities	13
Preparing the Consulting Services Agreement	16
Guidelines for Developing a Consulting Agreement	18
Guidelines for Budgeting	19
Leveraging Resources for Consulting Projects	19
Preparing the Statement of Work	20
Preparing Request for Proposal (RFP)	20
Assessing Proposals	22
Comparing Apples to Apples: Selecting the Right Consultant	23
The Pros and Cons of Consulting on the Clock	24
Contract Do's and Don'ts	26
Language in the Contract	27
The Contents of the Consulting Contract	29
The Ground Rules	33

Chapter 3: Working Side by Side with Your Consultant 35
Managing the Day-to-Day Relationship 35
Communication 36
The Importance of Guidance 39
Establishing a Collaborative Work Style 40
Building Trust into the Consulting Relationship ... 42

Chapter 4: Evaluating Outcomes and Making Adjustments 45
The "Rules of Engagement" 45
The 95-5 Rule 48
Keep it Simple 48
The Progress Report 49
The Fine Art of "Clienting" 53
Change Management 101 54
What to Do if Conflict Arises 56
Are We There Yet? Wrapping up the Work 58

Chapter 5: Consultant as Change Agent, Advocate, and Mentor 61
What Every Consultant Should Provide 61
Maximizing Consulting Value 63
Make Sure You're Learning to Fish 65
The Consulting Project Clinic 65
Knowledge Transfer and Tracking 68
What a Consultant Can Do That You Can't 69
Maximizing the Value of an Outside-Insider 70

Chapter 6: Consulting Dangers, Pitfalls, and Traps 73
Don't Accept "Cookie Cutter" Work 73
Beware of Arrogance (on Both Sides of the Table) ... 74
Put Expertise above Experience 76
Accountability for Results Starts with You 78
Advice-Based Consulting vs. Product-Based Consulting ... 80

Table of Contents

Chapter 7: Evaluating Your Consultant's Toolkit 83
Ten Great Questions Your Consultant Should Ask You........ 83
Debunking the Myths 88
Consultants are Paid to Rock the Boat.................................... 94
Stay Away from So-called Best Practices............................... 96

Chapter 8: Manager as Consultant 99
How to Be an Excellent Internal Consultant.......................... 100
Great Ideas Needed Greatly.. 100
The Art and Science of Consulting Creatively 101
The Power of Encouragement... 104
The Secret Sauce: Intellect Plus Intuition 105
Consultants and Managers Blazing the Trail Together.......... 107
The Next Chapter is Up to You 110

About the Author III

Introduction

A physician, a civil engineer, and a consultant were arguing about what was the oldest profession in the world.

The physician remarked, "Well, in the Bible, it says that God created Eve from a rib taken out of Adam. This clearly required surgery, and so I can rightly claim that mine is the oldest profession in the world."

The civil engineer interrupted, saying, "But even earlier in the book of Genesis, it states that God created the order of the heavens and the earth from out of the chaos. This was the first and certainly the most spectacular application of civil engineering. Therefore, good doctor, you are wrong: mine is the oldest profession in the world."

The consultant leaned back in her chair, smiled, and then said confidently, "Ah, but who do you think created the chaos?"

Problem 1: Most consultants take themselves too seriously, cost too much, stay too long, and don't play well with others.

Problem 2: Most managers dealing with consultants tend to be reactive and risk-averse, and are overwhelmed by all the mixed signals in this world of discontinuous change.

I bring a unique "3-D" perspective to what I call "the art of clienting": I've worked inside organizations *as the client*, I've worked externally as a *consultant*, and I've helped dozens of *other consultants* raise their game, get more clients, and deliver their highest value. Sitting on all three sides of the table, you learn a thing or two!

Of the thousands of people with whom I've spoken over the past 14 years, almost all agree on these three things: consulting and consultants have gotten a bad rap; consulting is not rocket science; and the practice of consulting is primarily about helping people solve specific problems or acquire and apply specific skills. Consulting is all about giving clients expert advice in an immediately understandable and useable package.

It's not about hiring a shadow workforce of hundreds of people doing the same work your employees are doing at quadruple the cost. And it's not about five-pound reports sitting on the CEO's shelf after she spent several hundred thousand dollars of hard-earned shareholders' money.

The approach outlined in this book is designed to help anyone who is responsible for delivering results for a company with, through—or sometimes in spite of—consultants:

- CEOs
- Vice presidents
- Managing directors
- Division managers
- Department managers
- Team leaders
- Key team players
- Entrepreneurs
- HR/Training and organizational development professionals
- Consultants

Chapter I
A Field Guide to Consultants

Wouldn't it be great if consultants came with an instruction manual?

There are many, many books written for consultants on how to work effectively with executives and managers inside client companies. However, most managers don't have the tools, strategies, and tips to maximize their end of the relationship and to take full advantage of the huge potential value that the *right* consultant—brought in for the *right* reason to do the *right* work the *right* way—can provide to their organizations. Until now.

What if the next consultant you hired came with an instruction manual—an instructional manual that is filled with strategies to maximize *your* end of the relationship and to take full advantage of what the *right* consultant can provide? You're holding that manual in your hand right now.

Managers who have to deal with consultants in addition to carrying out their own day-to-day work responsibilities feel understandably overwhelmed. This book will make the task less daunting.

Its purpose is to present practical how-to information about selecting the right consultant; maximizing the outcomes of their work; and making each consultant you work with "the best employee you never had to hire."

Consultants: Who They Are

A "consultant" is simply someone who gives expert or professional advice. In that respect, every employee in every organization qualifies as a consultant, though few think of themselves that way. I'll return to this notion in Chapter 8 to show you how, as a manager, your own consulting skills might be the most important of all.

For the purposes of getting started, though, let's focus on external consultants: experts in various fields who are brought into an organization to solve problems, address people issues, improve performance, provide process expertise, or contribute functional and technical knowledge and skills that the organization and its leadership deem necessary.

What Consultants Do

Before we outline the kinds of services an outside consultant can provide to a company or an organization, let's look at what a consultant considers to be his or her overall responsibility:

1. Define the problem.
2. Break it down.
3. Understand the business context.
4. Gather and analyze data.
5. Work with the client team.
6. Make recommendations.
7. Implement solutions.

Now let's go back to the general responsibilities any of these kinds of consultants tackle and get into more detail.

1. **Define the problem.** Work with the CEO or senior management team to identify the problem or issue they are facing and the desired goal.

2. **Break it down.** Work with the team to break the problem down into distinct parts, assign responsibilities, and develop hypotheses to provide a framework for the problem-solving process.

3. **Understand the business context.** Interview members of the client organization to understand how it operates, what the specific problems are and where they are, and identify data sources.

4. **Gather and analyze data.** Develop and refine models, analyze results, and refine hypotheses.

5. **Work with the client team.** Share early findings and engage in brainstorming and problem solving with client team members to lay the groundwork for effective implementation of recommendations. Communicate regularly with team members to build relationships and develop the trust necessary to act as counselors.

6. **Make recommendations.** Develop findings; evaluate possible solutions and determine recommendations; present results and recommendations to senior management.

7. **Implement solutions.** Roll up your sleeves. Do the work. Deliver the goods and measure results.

The Roles Consultants Play

A consultant is called upon to provide technical training, coaching, facilitating, or subject-matter expertise. Let's look at eight broad consultant roles:

Technical expert. A technical expert does not necessarily work with technology (although an IT consultant certainly does). I call a technical consultant an experienced "pair of hands" because his or her value is in the "been-there, done-that" expertise. Technical experts might include manufacturing experts, scientists, programmers, and engineers. Technical experts bring a proven step-by-step framework for exactly what to do, how to do it, when to do it, and when to make exceptions to the rules.

Mentor. *The Merriam-Webster's Collegiate Dictionary* defines a mentor as "a trusted counselor or guide." Sometimes a consultant is brought in to act as an older, wiser, more experienced individual who helps and guides another individual's development. Mentors usually work with clients individually, but can also mentor work groups, entire departments, or senior leadership teams.

Coach. A coach is someone who provides structure, accountability, and perspective and who will hold you to your commitments to move steadily forward toward your specific goals. Coaches provide insights that help clients find solutions more quickly and effectively than they could on their own. If you have a coach, you'll have someone to complain to or celebrate out loud with, and when you hit a roadblock, your coach will support you and guide you back into action.

Lecturer. Sometimes a consultant is brought in to be "messenger" of good or bad news, but the real purpose of having a so-called lecturer-consultant is to convey or explain information, news, concepts, and practices. In the best cases, lecturers provide highly concentrated and actionable information; in the worst cases, they deliver a dry, boring message or bad news that clients don't want to deliver themselves.

Trainer. Consultants can also be brought in to teach. In fact, the best consultants teach all the time, whether they're officially doing "training" or not. Training can take many forms, from frontline supervisory training to sales training, customer service training, leadership skills, negotiating, communication, executive education programs, technology training, regulatory training, product knowledge training, or motivational training.

Advisor. An advisor can act as a little bit of everything. For example, an advisor might act as part coach, part trainer, and part technical expert. An advisor's greatest asset is his/her experience; he or she provides a sounding board and seasoned advice when it comes to complex issues or difficult decisions.

Facilitator. Consultant-facilitators create arenas for managers, teams, and organizations to solve their own problems using a structured facilitation process. The skilled facilitator's main task is to help the group increase its effectiveness by improving processes and communication. Facilitators act in a neutral manner and make sure that everyone is heard; they resolve conflicts, they systematically work through issues, and they make sure that good decisions get made on the basis of complete information and inclusive opinion-sharing.

Subject Matter Expert (SME). Subject matter experts are humorously referred to as "brains for hire." That description is fairly accurate: These consultants have deep expertise in their subject matter. An SME might be a former professional in the same industry as their clients, or work in a totally unrelated field. Attorneys, medical doctors, labor negotiators, authors, university faculty, and Internet criminals–turned–security consultants are all in this category.

Alternatives to Using Consultants

You don't have to hire an outside consultant to do everything—particularly if you don't have an unlimited budget. One option is to contract out only portions of the project or study to consultants and have some tasks performed in-house. (This also helps an organization develop its internal capacity.) Management and staff do not necessarily need to be involved in the same project activities, however.

Here are some sample tasks that can be assigned in-house:

- Managers, staff members, key stakeholders, and/or partner organizations can conduct literature reviews or secondary research.
- Management and staff members (or even graduate students) can systematically examine available data or launch a survey to generate data.
- Staff members can integrate additional data collection into current service delivery mechanisms or products (send client questionnaires in each invoice, send employee surveys by e-mail, etc.).

When to Bring in a Consultant (and When *Not* To)

If you are thinking about hiring a consultant, be sure you really need an external resource. Here are the two basic questions that need to be answered if you are considering external consultants for any project:

1. Are there staff members with the required background, knowledge, and skills available within the organization to undertake the project?
2. Do you need to hire outside help in order to show the importance of the work, satisfy stakeholders, maintain objectivity (or the appearance of such), or for some other reason?

First, look at the expertise you already have. If your organization lacks specific experience or expertise, you can contract for that aspect of the work. In situations like this, it is wise to set up the contract so that there is some specific and measurable knowledge transfer to the internal staff by the end of the project.

Next, consider the desired outcomes and the target audience, as well as the risks associated with using an internal versus an external resource. Staff involvement in some project tasks might bias the results (e.g., tasks such as conducting focus groups, administering a survey on client satisfaction, establishing baseline numbers for a change initiative). For these specific tasks, external resources might be more appropriate.

For controversial programs where there has to be public accountability, you might have to employ an external consultant simply to eliminate any appearance of impropriety.

These are the questions you should ask yourself if you are still not sure you should hire an external consultant:

1. Are there sufficient funds designated for an external consulting project?
2. Has similar work been undertaken in-house? (e.g., previous iterations of similar programs)
3. Is there sufficient time and commitment to conduct the work?
4. Is the information or expertise available from other sources?
5. Are there existing measures or indicators of performance?
6. Will existing methods of information collection be useful for the purposes of this project?
7. Is there sufficient objectivity to conduct the work internally?
8. Is there anyone on staff who has training and experience in these specific project-related tasks?

Reasons to Use a Consultant

According to an *Entrepreneur* magazine survey, here are the top ten reasons organizations hire consultants:

1. Because of his or her expertise
2. To identify problems
3. To supplement staff expertise
4. To act as a catalyst to "get the ball rolling"
5. To provide much-needed objectivity
6. To teach
7. To do the "dirty work"
8. To bring new life to an organization
9. To create a new business
10. To influence other people

Key Questions to Ask a Prospective Consultant

I'm often asked by my clients, "What's the best way to make sure we hire the right people for key positions?" (They also sometimes ask me how to make sure they hire the best consultants, but I assure them that they've already done that!)

It's really pretty simple. Here are the two key questions you should ask a consultant before you hire them in order to tell the good consultants (and the not-so-good ones) from the great ones:

1. What would you do to solve this specific problem or challenge?
2. How would you implement your solution? What would it look like?

The best way for a consultant to present her skills to a prospective client is to pretend she has already been hired and start offering

Chapter 1: A Field Guide to Consultants

specific solutions. It's also a great way for companies to go about hiring customer service people, sales managers, top-level executives, and everyone in between.

There's been a lot of talk in the industry about "behavioral interviewing." This is a funny term, since so-called behavioral interviewing is not about behavior at all—it's just *talking* about behavior.

If you want a better way to gauge a prospective consultant's suitability to your organization and the task at hand, put them to work! That's right: After asking them the two questions about the position, have them spend a morning with you as if they had just been hired. Invite them to meetings, ask them to work with their prospective in-house teammates, have them call a customer or two, and ask them to do a short presentation for you. You'll learn a lot more than by asking silly rote questions.

Tip: For hiring both consultants and employees, replace the word *interview* with *audition*.

Chapter 2
Establishing the Relationship

Just as you cannot build a solid house without a foundation, you cannot build a solid consulting relationship without laying the foundation for it. Your preparation steps should include establishing roles and responsibilities (clearly and early on), and documenting the big-picture aims and the specific details of how the consulting relationship and the project itself is to unfold.

Preparing for the Consulting Project

The first task you should undertake to make sure that a successful consulting engagement takes place (and that you do the most effective *clienting* you possibly can) is to get your internal house in order. This means getting all the stakeholders, committees, and organizational leaders to buy in to and support the project for the right reasons, and with integrity and commitment.

Follow these two important steps to prepare for an outside consultant:

1. Establish roles and responsibilities.
2. Prepare the consulting services agreement (CSA).

Establishing Roles and Responsibilities

Project Coordinator. You will need to decide who the project coordinator will be before proceeding with the consulting work. He/she should be familiar with the project, understand the basics of the work at hand, and have good project-management skills.

Advisory Committee. You may also need to set up an advisory committee that comprises organizational and other stakeholder representatives (line managers, frontline employees, perhaps even customers, suppliers, and partners) who have an interest in the project or the organization.

It should be noted, however, that setting up an advisory committee tends to be very time- and resource-intensive for a small organization. Be sure you truly need an advisory committee. Small organizations should at least consider using existing work teams instead.

Tips for Setting up an Advisory Committee

- The roles and responsibilities of the advisory committee members should be clearly laid out.
- There should be one designated primary contact person on the committee.
- Outline methods and frequency of communication, and allow for ad-hoc meetings.
- Decide how formal committee documents will be prepared, distributed, and approved.
- Provide for review and amendment of the consulting agreement.

Steering Committee. A steering committee usually comprises senior managers, but it can also include central organizational representatives and regional representatives. When you want the advisory committee to have decision-making powers (i.e., final word on consulting deliverables), consider setting up a steering committee.

Deciding to Use an Advisory Committee, a Steering Committee, or Neither

When should you use an advisory committee?

When technical advice is needed and findings need to be situated within the overall context and organizational environment

When should you use a steering committee?

When you want to provide the opportunity for senior management to indicate its support for the project

When you want the committee to have decision-making powers

When the consulting project is high profile in nature

Advisory or steering committees might NOT be necessary in the following situations:

In a smaller organization where the manager or business owner who hires the consultant manages the relationship solo

When senior management has provided clear direction as to the project's expected goals and outcomes

When managers have a clear knowledge of the project's context, access to all appropriate sources of information, and the authority to implement the consulting recommendations in order to reach the expected goals and outcomes

Preparing the Consulting Services Agreement

Consulting agreements should include an overview of the consulting project and explicitly state management's initial requirements and expectations for the work at hand. They are useful tools for senior management in that they can guide the process until the consultant's scope of work or project plan becomes the primary document.

Consulting services agreements are used for many purposes:

- To engage senior managers and assure them that the consulting project will address their requirements
- To help manage the consulting work and the consultant
- To secure necessary stakeholder support
- To develop the consulting work plan

To prepare the consulting services agreement, begin by stating the following:

- Reasons for the consulting project
- Specific issues to be addressed
- Internal resources available for conducting the work
- Anticipated costs and the budget
- Expertise required to complete the project
- Time frame for completion

Chapter 2: Establishing the Relationship

Main Elements of a Consulting Services Agreement

Eight principal elements need to be included in every agreement for consulting services:

1. **Program Background**
   Program context and rationale
   Identification of key stakeholders, clients, and partners
   Program description

2. **Reasons for the Consulting Project**
   Statement of purpose
   Expected value-added
   Intended use of results

3. **Scope and Focus**
   Broad issues to be addressed/specific consulting questions
   Type of analysis to be used/level of detail
   The audience(s) for the reports and findings

4. **Statement of Work**
   How the purposes of the project are to be achieved
   Description of approaches
   Description of the data-collection methods to be used
   Listing of all the tasks required to undertake the project
   List of groups to be consulted
   Expectations with respect to communications and ongoing progress reports

5. **Consulting Team**
   Required professional qualifications/expertise/experience
   Roles and responsibilities of the consulting team itself and the organization's managers

6. **Timetable**
   Approximate timetable to guide the preparation of the work plan

7. **Budget**
   A specification of the estimated resources to be committed to the project and its components

8. **Deliverables**
   Identification of key deliverables (e.g., work plan or methodology report, assessment results, design documents, training manuals, specific events or initiatives, and hands-on implementation components of the work)

Guidelines for Developing a Consulting Agreement

- Be clear about the scope of the project and your expectations.
- Accurately describe the rationale for the initiative.
- Include specific consulting questions.
- Identify the separate manageable project tasks and the results that are expected.
- Do not assume that data sources will be available or accessible.
- Check to make sure the methodology is feasible.
- Clearly identify the specific abilities, qualifications, and skills required to carry out the project.
- Establish expectations for deliverables, work scheduling, and costs.
- Plan accordingly; writing up an agreement is time-consuming (i.e., two to five days).
- Read through other consulting agreements for ideas.

The consulting services agreement provides the basis for the next step in the process—selecting the consultant or consulting team.

There are four steps to the external-selection process:

1. Determine the sourcing options.
2. Identify the best value from potential candidates.
3. Notify the successful candidate.
4. Negotiate and sign the contract.

Consultants will often have questions about the services agreement. Designate one contact person to coordinate the responses to these questions, and be sure that you provide the same information to all consultants. Fax or e-mail all your responses to each candidate.

Guidelines for Budgeting

Budgeting for consulting projects should be part of the upfront planning. It is important to specify a budget amount or range in the agreement. This will help you judge which proposals offer the best value per dollar.

Budgeting usually means breaking down the project into components or tasks and providing financial estimates for each component. You can consider costs related to internal staff, consultants, travel, communications, printing and photocopying, supplies and equipment, meetings, seminars, and events:

- Consider costs of previous or similar consulting work.
- Consider the trade-off between consulting experience/quality and budget.
- Earmark about 25 percent for data collection and use the remainder of the money for project design, implementation, and reporting.

Leveraging Resources for Consulting Projects

A smaller organization can supplement its limited resources by leveraging its needs and resources. While not all strategies will be applicable to your organization, here are some suggestions:

- Group external and internal data collection and analysis tasks as much as possible to avoid redundancy and achieve economies of scale.
- Search for extra funding from departments or groups with a stake in the outcome (e.g., women's issues, diversity initiatives, or quality certification projects).
- Conduct consulting work with organizational "partners" who are involved in the same issues or initiatives.

- Collaborate with partner organizations to pre-qualify consultants and form a pool of readily available and experienced people who can help reduce the administrative burdens of contracting and provide you with top quality and proven talent.

Preparing the Statement of Work

The "statement of work" is the main agreement between the manager and the consultant, and it is always a written agreement. The consultant responds to this document by developing a work plan that outlines the study purpose and objectives, approach, methods of data collection, and tasks.

You will need to decide how much detail to put in the statement of work. You might prefer to make the statement of work less detailed and rely on the consultant to suggest specific approaches and methodologies. However, a detailed statement gives prospective consultants a better idea of your expectations (and consultants can always suggest changes to approach and methods). Ask candidates to discuss possible methodological challenges and solutions; this can help you assess the consultant's expertise. It will also serve to strengthen the proposed work plan.

Preparing Request for Proposal (RFP)

Developing a well-written RFP takes time and planning. However, when it is completed, it provides a common format so that you can more easily compare proposals (which will make your job much easier when it comes to selecting a qualified consultant). The information that follows will help you develop a consistent approach to requesting proposals from outside resources.

Chapter 2: Establishing the Relationship

Typical Components of an RFP

Organizational Overview: Company overview, management profile of principals, areas of specialty, publications, and other qualifications and unique characteristics of the firm or individual.

Program Description: A high-level overview of the services, expertise, and deliverables you're looking for.

Target Audience: A description of the internal staff members who will be interfacing with the consulting team (e.g., will the consultant be working with entry-level sales people, senior executives, or call-center managers and teams?).

Required Deliverables: What items do you want the consultant to create, develop, deliver, or collaborate with you on (e.g., process maps, employee survey design and delivery, executive education seminars, or a marketing operations manual for a new product/service)?

Assumptions and Agreements: Deadlines by which the project must be complete; preliminary budget projections for each phase of the work; approval mechanisms; project team reporting structure; desired technical support and follow-up activities; knowledge transfer requirements; intellectual property ownership of consultant-developed materials; travel and lodging expense reimbursement; billing mechanisms; payment terms; and anything else that you would like to spell out to clarify how you prefer to work with outside resources. (Hint: You will rarely go wrong by putting too much information into the Assumptions and Agreements section!)

Format: Where you specify your desired format for the consultant's proposal document (e.g., you might request that proposals contain a technical section and a time-cost section).

In the technical section, the consultant should include time lines, projected required personnel, and schedules for completing the project.

In the time-cost section, the consultant should detail the time and costs that will be required to complete the project, including any options.

(continued)

The Manager's Pocket Guide to Using Consultants

> **Typical Components of an RFP** *(concluded)*
>
> **Additional Documentation (optional):** A free-form area where consultants can include other supporting documentation (e.g., a demo video, audio CD, testimonial sheet, relevant newspaper articles, or books they've published on the subject at hand).
>
> **Request for References (optional):** You might want to ask the consultant to provide client references that you can contact in order to assess the qualifications, fit, and level of success of the consultant.
>
> **Submission Deadline and Address:** Specify the deadline for consideration and the specific name and address to which the consultant should send their materials. It is also helpful to provide the name of a contact person who can answer questions and clarify the terms of the RFP.
>
> **Award Date:** Specify the time frame for making a selection and notification.

Assessing Proposals

Proposals are commonly assessed based on one of these categories:

1. **The lowest price.** This method is often used when cost is the most important factor, or when hard requirements are the main tool for evaluating the proposals, and when suppliers offer uniform services.

2. **The best technical proposal.** The proposal that receives the highest score within the budget is the winner here. This method is often used when technical merit is the most important factor. A maximum budget is identified in the RFP; point-rated requirements are typically used to assess proposals.

3. **The best overall value for the money.** The proposal that has the best ratio of desired value and deliverables to price is the winning proposal here. This method is used when technical merit and price are both important factors.

> **Things to Consider When Reviewing Proposals**
>
> Qualifications of the consulting team
>
> Professional background and experience (e.g., relevant industry or client experience)
>
> Personal qualities: ability to communicate, teamwork capabilities, leadership skills (Note: leadership skills are particularly important when dealing with numerous stakeholders and partners, especially at senior levels)
>
> Consulting skills (e.g., knowledge and practical application of consulting methodologies)
>
> Subject matter expertise
>
> Demonstrated performance levels (check references)
>
> Avoid boiler-plate solutions; the approach proposed should be relevant to the needs of your organization and be as customized as possible; bidders should demonstrate an understanding of your organization's specific needs and challenges
>
> Demonstrated ability to do the project within the designated time frame
>
> Soundness of methodology and work plan
>
> Demonstrated understanding of challenges and methodological limitations
>
> Balance of junior and senior consultants with minimal "on the job" training
>
> Existence of qualified back-up personnel (particularly important when using smaller firms)

Comparing Apples to Apples: Selecting the Right Consultant

A small sample of tips to get your thinking started:

- A consultant's value is directly related to the ideas and answers he or she brings to a business situation that other individuals won't, don't, or can't.

- Select a consultant based on *expertise,* not just *experience.* A prospective consultant might have spent his or her whole career in your industry doing merely average work. Is that really someone you want on your team?

- Assess personality, style, and overall fit, not just credentials and track record. For example, a brilliant Ivy-league MBA with impeccable Fortune 500 references might have a very hard time making profitable changes in a tightly controlled family business environment.

Generate a short list on paper of all the consultants and consulting firms in the final running. And then always, *always* meet the consultants face to face so that you can supplement your intellectual data with your intuitive reactions to them as people. The relationship *will not* get more comfortable as time goes on if it doesn't feel right at the outset.

The Pros and Cons of Consulting on the Clock

Consultant Alan Weiss believes that clients and consultants short-change themselves if they bill by the hour. He says there are ten reasons why a client should insist on value-based billing rather than time-based billing in his article, "Ten Ways to Convince a Buyer That Value-Based Fees Are Best" (www.summitconsulting.com). Here they are, in his words:

1. There is a cap on your investment. You know exactly what is to be spent, and there are no surprises.

2. There is never a "meter running."

3. It is unfair to you to place you in the position of having to make an investment decision every time you need my help.

Chapter 2: Establishing the Relationship

Otherwise, you're trying to determine the impossible: Is this an issue that justifies a $2,000 visit, or a $500 phone call? No client should ever be in that position.

4. Your people should feel free to use my assistance and to ask for my help without feeling they have to go to someone for budgetary approval. This only makes them more resistant to sharing their views, and at best delays the flow of important information.

5. If I find additional work that was unanticipated but must be performed, I can do it without having to come to you for additional funds. In those instances, legitimate, additional work would otherwise be viewed as self-aggrandizing and an attempt to generate additional hours or days.

6. If you find additional, related work that must be done, you can freely request it without worry about increased costs.

7. The overall, set fee, in relation to the project outcomes to be delivered, is inevitably less of a proportional investment than hourly billing.

8. If conditions change in your organization, you won't be in the difficult situation of having to request that the project be completed in less time. The quality approach is assured, since the fee is set and paid.

9. If I decide that additional resources are necessary, there is no cost to you and I can employ additional help as I see fit.

10. This is the most uncomplicated way to work together. There will never be a debate about what is billable time (e.g., travel, report writing) or what should be done on site or off site.

On the other side of the coin, sometimes you need a "single sniper," rather than a "fully loaded tank."

Consider using hourly billing in the following cases:

1. The project is fairly small in scope and/or it needs outside specialized expertise for only a short amount of time.

2. You want to keep a firm "hand on the wheel" and control exactly how much outside help you need, when, and for what specific aspects of the work.

3. During a longer, more protracted project, you want to keep a consultant motivated and 100 percent focused on delivering the goods at the beginning, the middle, and the end of the work. (Value-based billing sometimes leads to complacency and a lowered priority for your project—after all, it's already paid for!)

4. You or your management team is entrenched in a "pay-for-hours" mindset, and moving off that model would reduce your internal buy-in for the project altogether.

5. Cash flow considerations—you don't want to spend a large amount of upfront money, and would rather spend more money over time rather than pay a fixed value-based fee in a lump sum.

6. You're not sure of the consultant's "fit" for your project and want to adopt a "pay-as-you-go" phased-work model and cut your losses if things don't work out early on.

Contract Do's and Don'ts

Consulting agreements are contracts. Contracts differ from informal agreements in that contracts create binding obligations between parties. Contracts have definite legal consequences, so client organizations and consultants have to understand the legal nature of the contractual relationship they are creating. You will want to obtain legal advice before finalizing any consulting agreement or contract.

This may be obvious, but it's worth mentioning: Before signing an agreement with the consultant, you must make sure that:

- You understand and agree to every term and condition of the contract.
- Your consultant understands and agrees to every term and condition of the contract.

Contracts should never be signed quickly or without careful consideration. The time and money spent on legal fees arising from poorly considered contracts by far exceed the upfront time and money that it takes to be sure that both parties are truly in agreement on all aspects of the nature of the project, the relationship, and the specific details of the written contract.

Let's look at the consulting contract in two parts: the language in the contract, and what the contract should contain.

Language in the Contract

Make sure your contracts are clearly and precisely written. Each party should know precisely what is expected of him or her. The rights and obligations under the contract should not only be apparent to the parties, but also be clear to any objective outsider who reads the agreement. Contracts that are vague and imprecise are likely to lead to legal action.

Expressed and implied terms. "Expressed" terms are those terms that are stated in words in the agreement itself. "Implied" terms are those that do not appear in the wording of the agreement itself, but are deduced from the expressed wording and surrounding circumstances by necessary implication. They are terms that are so obvious that the parties did not see a need to express them in writing. For instance, an agreement to buy a car does not have to state expressly that the car has to have an engine, four wheels, and seats, since this is necessarily implied.

You should express your intentions as clearly as possible; do not rely too much on what you think the other party understands.

Misrepresentation. A misrepresentation is a false statement of fact made by one party that induced or persuaded the other to agree to. Misrepresentation can be either *fraudulent* or *negligent*. *Fraudulent misrepresentation* occurs when the guilty party makes a false statement of fact with the intention of deceiving the other party. (For example, a consultant who makes false representations about his or her qualifications or experience might manage to convince the client organization to award the contract to him or her.) A *negligent misrepresentation* is a false statement of fact made without the intention to mislead. If you discover that the consultant made a misrepresentation (fraudulently or negligently), you should consider the following:

> Has the misrepresentation induced you to enter into the agreement? In other words, would the consultant still have been awarded the contract if the truth was known? If the answer to this question is no, decide to abide by the agreement (or rescind it). Then inform the other party of your decision within a reasonable time of making the discovery. If you do not do this, it can be inferred that you decided to abide by the contract.

Mistakes. It is not unusual for one or both parties to be mistaken about some aspect of the contract. Mistakes can either be unilateral (only one party is operating under the mistaken assumption) or common (both parties operate under the same mistake).

Trivial mistakes have no effect on a contract because the mistaken party would have concluded the same contract even if the mistake has been discovered before the contract was concluded.

Material mistakes relate to essential terms or conditions of the contract. For example, one party thought he was purchasing a

Mercedes, whereas the other party intended to sell a Volkswagen Beetle. A material mistake prevents the parties from reaching true consensus and thus nullifies the contract.

Make sure that both you and the consultant understand every aspect of the agreement and that you share the same understanding of the agreement. Before signing, read the agreement carefully to make sure that it correctly reflects your true intentions.

Changes. As a general rule, the parties to an agreement are free to change the terms of the contract, and they often do. However, if the contract specifies that changes should be done in a particular way, the parties must follow that procedure in order for the change to be valid. (For instance, a contract may contain a non-variation clause that states that any variation to the agreement has to be written down and signed by both parties. In such a case, it is obviously impossible to change the terms of the contract verbally.)

If you agree to amend the consulting agreement (however minor the change), always make sure that the amendment is written into the contract or attached and signed by you and the consultant. A "gentleman's agreement" is not enough.

The Contents of the Consulting Contract

Here are the main components in a contract between the client and the consultant:

The definition clause (or interpretation clause). This clause serves two main functions: to define the meaning attached to key words and phrases that appear throughout the contract, and to ensure that the same meaning is attached to those words or phrases throughout the contract. Typically, the definition clause states that "The following words or phrases that appear in this agreement bear the meaning assigned to them in this section:

'The Consultant' means Federal Widget Consulting LLC

'The Client' means the Government of the United States

'The Department' means the Department of Health

'The parties' means the parties to this agreement

'The Consulting Services Agreement' or 'CSA' means the Consulting Services Agreement annexed hereto as Schedule A."

Warranties. Contracts are usually awarded to consultants on the basis of their skill, qualifications, knowledge, and general know-how, usually as a result of representations made by the consultant that he/she is qualified to perform the assignment. It's always a good idea to include a clause in the agreement in which the consultant warrants his or her abilities to perform the task. Such a clause could state the following:

WARRANTIES: The consultant warrants that he or she has the requisite experience, knowledge, stated professional certifications, and skill to perform the assignment as set out in the Consulting Services Agreement. This warranty constitutes a material representation of fact, which induced the organization to award the contract to the consultant.

If it becomes apparent later that the consultant is incapable of performing the assignment as required or has falsely represented any credentials, the contract can be terminated on the basis of misrepresentation.

The duration of the contract. The agreement should specify both the commencement date and the termination date of the contract. It can also state that the contract may be extended by a further period (for example, six months) by agreement in writing and signed by both parties. Unless the contract is extended by agreement between the parties, it terminates on the termination date.

Duties of the client organization. The client organization that hires the consultant has a duty to provide the consultant with assistance reasonably required for the completion of the assignment, including all information, diagrams, reports, or contracts that are relevant to the completion of the assignment.

Duties of the consultant. The duties of the consultant should include but are not limited to the following:

- **Reporting.** The consultant should be required to provide a comprehensive report on the assignment by a specific date. The clause should state how the report is to be arranged (including the main headings), how recommendations are to be set out, financial evaluation, and so on. The report that the consultant produces is a fundamental aspect of his or her service delivery, as it lays the basis for far-reaching decisions made by the client organization. You must therefore be clear as to what you hope to achieve with the report, and you should insist on clarity and conciseness in the drafting of the report.

- **Records.** The consultant should be required to keep records of all expenses and accounts, and to make these available to the client upon request.

- **Confidentiality.** The consultant should treat as confidential any information supplied to him or her by the client organization or that is otherwise obtained in connection with the agreement. Furthermore, the report that the consultant is required to draft should be confidential; the consultant should not publish or discuss any aspect of the report, or any information that he or she acquires as a result of the contract, unless this is done with the written permission of the client.

Payment. The payment clause should explain how and when payments will be made. The payment clause should also make provision for the payment of expenses (travel, accommodation, etc.) upon presentation of original invoices and receipts.

Intellectual property. This clause should state that all intellectual property rights obtained by the consultant in connection with the agreement belong to your organization, that all documents prepared by the consultant are the exclusive property of the client organization, and that the consultant may only use them for purposes unrelated to the agreement with the written consent of the client.

Indemnity. This clause should stipulate that your organization shall not in any way be liable for any damage or losses suffered by any person arising out of any act or omission of your consultant. This clause serves to protect your organization if your consultant (knowingly or not) violates any laws or breaches any of the rights of third parties in performing his or her duties.

Subcontracting. This clause should specify that the consultant may not subcontract any aspect of the assignment to third parties without the written consent of the client organization; that written consent to allow subcontracting will in no way discharge the consultant of any obligation in terms of the agreement; and that the third party (subcontractor) will not have any claim against your organization arising out of the agreement between himself or herself and the consultant.

Training and development. The agreement may specify that the consultant shall provide training for the client organization's employees assigned to him or her in areas identified by the organization and that arise from the delivery of services in accordance with the agreement. This clause will facilitate skills transfer between the consultant and your organization, thus increasing your own team's capacity to undertake similar assignments in the future.

Termination of the agreement. This clause can stipulate that either party may terminate the agreement in the event of a material breach by the other party or by giving one month's written notice of his or her intention to do so.

Penalty clause. This clause introduces a penalty for failure to deliver the required service in a timely manner. For example, the penalty might take the form of a deduction of a percentage of the amount payable for every day that the service is overdue.

Resolution of disputes. This clause should stipulate that any dispute arising from the agreement should be settled through a process of mediation. Should the mediation process prove to be unsuccessful, the matter should be referred to arbitration.

Appendices. The consulting contract can contain several appendices. Appendices should always be clearly marked as Appendix A, B, C, and so on. Appendices should be referred to and explained in the body of the contract itself. Appendices that are attached without explanation create confusion about their relevance. Reference to an appendix should be made in the following way: "The consultant agrees to conduct interviews with managers in the department listed in Appendix A to this agreement." Appendices are not separate documents from the consulting contract; rather, they form an integral component of the contract. Thus, failure to comply with requirements, specifications, or conditions listed in an appendix can be regarded as a breach of contract.

The Ground Rules

No matter who you end up working with or how you decide to compensate them, there are some very basic ground rules that you should establish when working with any outside resource.

Ground rules govern the functional ways and means of engagement. We are not always good at communicating with one another, but the ground rules we create, commit to, and follow will help us build and strengthen healthy working relationships.

Ground Rules for Consultant and Client

- Test assumptions and inferences.
- Share all relevant information.
- Focus on interests, not positions.
- Be specific—use examples.
- Focus on issues, not personalities.
- Agree on what important words mean.
- Explain the reasons behind one's statements, questions, and actions.
- Disagree openly and with respect (no hidden agendas).
- Make statements, then invite questions and comments.
- Jointly design ways to test disagreements and solutions.
- Discuss "undiscussable" issues.
- Clarify and refine expectations on both sides.
- Keep the discussion focused.
- Do not take cheap shots.
- All members are expected to participate in all phases of the process.
- Exchange relevant information with all interested parties. Make decisions by consensus.
- Do frequent self-critiques and debriefs.
- Keep what's shared confidential.
- Show up to meetings on time.
- Listen actively and respect others when they are talking.
- Be conscious of body language and nonverbal responses. They can be as disrespectful as words.

Chapter 3
Working Side by Side with Your Consultant

As work begins, managing the consulting relationship, establishing healthy two-way communication patterns, and developing mutual trust will become the manager's critical tasks. These are things that definitely will *not* take care of themselves; to ignore them is to commit management abdication. Keep in mind that a good consultant will be doing the project *with* you, and not *to* you. It's important for you as the manager to stay in the game and play smart, so both you and your consultant win.

Managing the Day-to-Day Relationship

The relationship between the consultant and the manager is a partnership: You bring subject matter expertise and he or she brings consulting or process expertise. However, the manager's main role is to make sure that the consultant follows the agreed-upon work plan and provides a satisfactory level of quality.

The manager must also address issues that the consultant raises when preparing and implementing the work plan. While there is no single good strategy for managing consultants, here are some good recommendations.

> ### The Client-Consultant Relationship
>
> Use these guidelines to create a solid and effective manager-consultant relationship:
>
> 1. Set realistic time frames for deliverables.
> 2. Maintain an active role in the project.
> 3. Anticipate what might go wrong, and develop strategies to deal with it.
> 4. Keep formal and informal lines of communication open. You should have a good sense of the status of the project at all times (i.e., status of data collection, status of preliminary findings).
> 5. Establish a positive working relationship.
> 6. In addition to regular meetings and other contacts, keep the project on track through interim reports.
> 7. Regularly check on the progress of the work.
> 8. Realize that it is not unusual to have problems or misunderstandings during a project.
> 9. Address problems as quickly as they arise.
> 10. Discuss any deviations from the consulting services agreement.
> 11. Provide timely and considered reviews of all reports (e.g., methodology reports, interim, and final) and ask questions.
> 12. Keep key stakeholders informed about the progress of the project.
> 13. Make sure that there is sufficient time to review draft and final reports.

Communication

It is best to establish a regular flow of communication with your consultant or consulting team.

You do not need to have formal sit-down meetings, but be sure to communicate openly and directly through any of the following:

- E-mail
- Status reports

Chapter 3: Working Side by Side with Your Consultant

- Direct phone conversations
- Group conference calls
- The company intranet (posting updates, questions, or issues)
- Virtual meetings using computer or video technology
- Live in-person meetings

Managers can't do everything themselves, so they **delegate** their authority to people who can accomplish tasks for them. This means more than simply assigning tasks.

Keep the following in mind when you work with consultants:

Delegation empowers people to work without having to have detailed instructions or close supervision. While it involves some risk, delegation unleashes motivation and creativity by allowing the individual people to act as their own boss.

There are obligations. Delegation implies that while one is empowered to do the job, he is also held responsible and accountable for results:

- "Responsible" in that he or she has an obligation to perform the duties of one's position and achieve objectives.
- "Accountable" in that he or she has an obligation to answer for results (how well he or she has performed).

Caution: A manager can delegate authority, but cannot delegate or mandate personal responsibility or accountability. Though he can hold employees and consultants responsible and accountable within their areas, he's still ultimately responsible for their performance. Any manager who shifts personal responsibility or accountability onto subordinates (or consultants) is guilty of abdication.

If you don't delegate. If managers don't delegate, they'll stay fully involved in their employees' work or will end up doing it themselves. If they simply assign work and provide no latitude or resources or they meddle or micro-manage, they are not delegating. Managers who don't delegate usually work hard, measuring success by the effort they have exerted and the hours they've worked. They have worked hard but not worked smart, and they thus achieve little of value. The main reason they fail is that they won't delegate.

Delegation can lead to success. Effective managers realize that delegation is their most powerful management tool. They measure their success by the results their employees and their consultants produce. They empower people and treat them as adults, knowing that they'll act responsibly without need for constant checking. Delegation raises employee's stature from mere "hired hands" or "order takers" to valued team members and partners.

In your day-to-day work with consultants, it is important to balance authority, responsibility, and accountability.

Examples of balance in a delegated task:

Authority	— Enough to fulfill responsibility and maintain accountability (neither too much nor too little)
	— Sufficient resources and autonomy to make decisions
Responsibility	— Able to use one's talents and make the job challenging
	— A manageable workload so that you don't have to work to exhaustion
	— Not set up to fail
Accountability	— Realistic, worthy, and attainable standards
	— Zero tolerance for poor performance
	— Reward for excellent performance

Chapter 3: Working Side by Side with Your Consultant

Examples of Imbalance	
If the manager . . .	**then the employee or consultant . . .**
• delegates too much authority	• might get out of control
• doesn't delegate enough authority	• might work to exhaustion and still fail
• assigns too much responsibility	• will not accomplish everything
• assigns too little responsibility	• won't perform to full capacity
• demands impossible results	• will fail
• doesn't demand accountability	• will get away with poor performance

The Importance of Guidance

When we use the term *guidance* we are basically talking about information or advice that a manager provides when assigning tasks—a broad form of direction that encourages self-reliance and initiative.

Most managers appreciate employees who can work without detailed instructions and close supervision. Rather than giving details on how they want something done, they issue guidelines for what they want done. Proper guidance removes constraints of detailed instructions and close supervision. This sets both employees and consultants free to pursue innovative solutions.

> ### Guidance and Delegation
>
> Delegating details and procedures allows a manager to avoid micromanaging and focus on larger issues. Providing only broad guidance to a consultant has several advantages. It:
>
> - Eliminates need for close supervision
> - Provides flexibility to choose the means for accomplishing the task
> - Encourages initiative
> - Builds morale and self-confidence
> - Unleashes creativity
> - Leads to imaginative solutions
> - Promotes personal growth
>
> **The degree of guidance one seeks or provides depends on factors such as:**
> - Personal expertise and experience
> - Available information and other resources
> - Complexity of the task
> - The manager's leadership style
>
> **Areas where the manager should provide guidance:**
> - Desired results
> - Conditions a solution must satisfy
> - Things that must not go wrong
> - What must remain unchanged
> - Resource constraints
> - Budget constraints
> - Acceptable alternatives
> - People to contact
> - Political or protocol considerations
> - Sources of possible contention or conflict

Establishing a Collaborative Work Style

The most important factor in effectively maximizing the potential contribution of a consultant is the manager-consultant relationship. If you establish a collaborative relationship early on, every bump in the road will be minimized and every milestone will be a mutual success.

Chapter 3: Working Side by Side with Your Consultant

Why collaborate? Because that's the only way you will survive. Increasing levels of project complexity require expertise in highly specialized fields. Time itself has become a commodity, and the net result is a flattening of organizational structures—high-stakes decision making, once the hallmark of high-level executives, is now in the hands of managers and consultants working on the front lines.

Despite the high stakes, professional collaboration is still not well understood by most managers and executives. Michael Schrage pointed out in his 1989 book *No More Teams!* that simply tasking people to work together is not true collaboration, and might not even result in a collaborative and productive relationship. Schrage says that highly effective teams have four key elements: (1) one or more compelling, shared goals; (2) team members with unique competencies that will contribute to successful outcomes; (3) members who operate within a formal structure, with defined roles that facilitate collective/collaborative work; and (4) mutual respect, tolerance, and trust.

> ### The Characteristics of Managers
> ### Who Are Adept at Teaming and Collaboration
>
> **Personally**
> - Are willing and able to take on different roles and tasks to accomplish shared ends
> - Are open and honest with ideas, concerns, and values
> - Are leaders as well as followers
> - Apply collaborative skills to a variety of situations
> - Reflect on group interactions after collaborative activities and use these experiences to make future collaboration more productive
>
> **Interpersonally**
> - Commit to a shared goal and accept responsibility for group work toward that goal
> - Work to match tasks to team member abilities, expanding team membership when necessary
> - Share personal understandings and resources with other group members
> - Listen respectfully and objectively; offer constructive feedback
> - Iteratively design and redesign solutions through honest debate, disagreement, discussion, research, and development

Building Trust into the Consulting Relationship

When trust is lacking in a consulting relationship, all sorts of obstacles begin to get in the way of the work. Information is hoarded when it should be shared. Communication slows down when it should be accelerating. Problems are concealed when they should be exposed and collaboratively solved. Collaboration and creativity are replaced with resistance, cynicism, and fear. Overall, it becomes a pretty bad situation.

Here are some things to think about as you build trusting relationships with colleagues, employees, and consultants. Make sure they start healthy and stay healthy.

Chapter 3: Working Side by Side with Your Consultant

1. **Trusting relationships are built on an even playing field.** People must view each other as equally important in the relationship. It is especially important that managers and consultants start off as peers. Be willing to share information, even about yourself. Conversely, seek out information about your consultant and a little bit about what makes him or her "tick." This is the first step in establishing a healthy, trusting relationship.

2. **Needs should be communicated and acted upon.** Every relationship is about getting needs met. After all, needs are one of the main reasons you enter into consulting relationships in the first place. Ask what your consultant needs, and communicate your own needs clearly, assertively, and with a positive spirit. Act on what you hear, and deliver on what you say. This consistency and congruence is another critical building block of a high-trust relationship.

3. **Time and attention are required to build trusting relationships.** Some relationships require more care and feeding than others, but no relationship can grow and thrive unless there is time set aside for collaboration, communication, and the building of mutual understanding. The last thing you may have time for is one more meeting or one more to-do item, but it is vitally important that you make the time to build a strong relationship with your consulting resource.

4. **Consultants and managers need to feel safe with each other.** Emotional and psychological safety is what we get when there is trust between two people. It is this safety that allows weaknesses to be shared, problems to be raised, and concerns to be voiced. It is also this safety that allows you, as the manager, to proactively stay involved at every phase of the consulting project, give your authentic input, and help co-pilot the consulting project to its ultimate successful

conclusion. Make sure that people know they can count on your respect and your loyalty, unless and until they prove themselves undeserving.

5. **Differences should be accepted and respected.** It goes without saying that one of the reasons your consultant was brought in was to take advantage of their differences—different skills, different attitudes, different perspectives, and different capabilities. These are by no means "better" or "more valuable" than your own—just different. Both you and your consultant should feel comfortable being yourselves. Express your thoughts, ideas, and feelings, even if they differ. The key is to remember that when differences arise, we don't judge, don't criticize, and don't reject the other person for the difference. Instead, we explore the difference and extract the greatest value from it, free of ego considerations, and without adversarial attitudes. Be open and willing to be influenced.

Chapter 4
Evaluating Outcomes and Making Adjustments

A game where you don't keep score is a game not worth playing. In fact, the word for playing without keeping score is *practice*. But the projects you're working on are all too real, so it's critical that you take the pulse of the project frequently, and measure results along the way. This is the only way to make wise midstream corrections, stay on course, and ensure that you and your organization arrive at your destination in the shortest possible time and with the least possible expense. Measuring progress, managing conflict, skillfully navigating change, and gracefully wrapping up are all part of bringing your project to a successful and profitable close.

The "Rules of Engagement"

There are rules that every manager—and every consultant—would be wise to consider before embarking on a consulting project. I call them the Nine Rules of Engagement.

Rule 1: Outcome, outcome, outcome. Consultants generally get hired because they sell the outcome of the project, not the features or the benefits or the methodologies or the approaches. Now that work is beginning, make sure that everyone agrees with your clear and specific (and hopefully measurable) statement of outcomes. Make it explicit, and write it down. Kick off the first meeting by discussing it and gaining agreement.

Rule 2: Build the best team you can. Consultants rarely work alone. As a manager, make sure your virtual Rolodex is full of good people you can rely on who complement the skills of your own internal team. Then tap in to as many of those internal resources as you can so that the work is a seamless collaboration with a good balance of inside and outside perspectives.

Rule 3: Create a roadmap and stick to it. A smart manager always maps out a plan. It doesn't have to be formal or fancy, but it does have to lay out the major phases of the work, the checkpoints, and the results that the organization expects after every major checkpoint. Make sure to revise the roadmap as your consultant's work progresses and make adjustments. Then continually communicate progress in both directions in terms of the updated map.

Rule 4: Don't bite off more than you can chew. This applies to consultants and managers alike. Remain focused on priorities, and try to accomplish a series of smaller projects. Get enthusiastic senior management buy-in after each phase. Remember Einstein's words of wisdom: "The reason time exists is so that everything doesn't happen all at once."

Rule 5: Consulting is a "people" business. Every business relationship is a personal relationship. Remember to accommodate people's needs and priorities. Make other people look good! Relationships are everything; nothing you say or do will matter if people don't trust and respect you.

Rule 6: Buy in and stay in. Make sure to go beyond getting "senior management approval" for your project. Ideally, you want hysterical management enthusiasm. When that is not possible, the minimum buy-in is a clear and explicit conceptual agreement on

Chapter 4: Evaluating Outcomes and Making Adjustments

the destination (where we are going), the roadmap (how and when we will get there), the outcomes (what this will look like when we're done), and the bottom-line value of the project (why we are doing this, and how much money this will make or save). Stay-in is the ongoing process of communication, and it's vital if you want the continuing interest and enthusiasm of all stakeholders (especially if you are working on a long-term project).

Rule 7: Be willing to change. Being open to change means remaining flexible and light on your feet. Changes can happen for a variety of reasons: learning new information, changing market conditions, finding the problem behind the problem, and so on. And sometimes, consultants change things for their own reasons. Whatever the cause, a shrewd manager recognizes when change is needed, knows how to introduce changes effectively ("surf the wave"), and knows how to proactively communicate the impact of changes in positive, outcome-focused terms.

Rule 8: Communicate, communicate, communicate. You must keep all stakeholders informed. This is very important! Make sure you clearly communicate what you're doing. Project management expert Robert Graham developed what is referred to as Graham's Law: "If they know nothing of what you are doing, they suspect you are doing nothing." Of course, this bit of advice applies equally to consultants!

Rule 9: A consultant is a leader. A consultant is a *de facto* leader, not merely a hired hand. A consultant's own leadership skills will be needed to motivate people, come up with creative, useful solutions, apply expertise to complex problems, teach, mentor, challenge, empower, inspire, delegate, communicate, and mobilize.

The 95-5 Rule

Have you ever heard of the 95-5 Rule? It goes like this: About 95 percent of problems, symptoms, issues, and challenges can be effectively addressed by making significant changes to only 5 percent of the processes, the people, or the technology. Focus like a laser beam on the 5 percent of the solution that can make a real difference *right now.*

Keep it Simple

Let me take a moment to define the way I'm using the word *simple*. I am not referring to something simplistic or common or easy, but rather the *shortest way* to the *best answer*. A lot of consultants and managers end up, for whatever reason, taking the exact opposite route—the most complicated way to a workable answer. Workable isn't good enough. People are expecting brilliant, remarkable, ingenious, and—you guessed it—simple.

The way you can tell you've hit the mark is when someone says something like, "I can't believe the results from these few simple changes. This would never have occurred to me!" Bingo. Keep it simple. It is often the quickest and cheapest solution. And simple often gets the job done.

It's easy to take something simple and make it complicated. What's hard is to take something complicated and simplify it.

Chapter 4: Evaluating Outcomes and Making Adjustments

> **Try this . . .**
>
> - Think effectiveness, not efficiency.
>
>   Efficiency = "We're here for 60 hours, so let's make the most of it."
>
>   Effectiveness = "How quickly can we make real improvements today, this week, this month, that will last long after we're done?"
> - It doesn't matter how hard you work or how brilliant your solutions if you're working on the wrong pieces of the puzzle.
> - Use systems thinking: Look for connections and dependencies, talk to all sorts of people, and allow that information to direct you to the critical 5 percent where you can leverage the most from your work.
> - Ask "dumb" questions.
> - Breakthrough insights come from having a fresh pair of eyes and ears.
> - Investigate the basics, and you'll be amazed at what you find.

The Progress Report

Set up a process to check on the work that is being done. One way to keep both manager and consultant informed of where things are and what needs to be done in relation to the "big picture" destination is to prepare a progress report. This important two-way communication tool usually covers the vision, initiatives, accomplishments to date, and the status of various project tasks, and a list of what is still to be done. Let's look at each part of the progress report in more detail.

Introduction/vision. A brief one to two paragraph overview of the project itself—its context, purpose, and desired outcomes. This is often taken directly from the Request for Proposal or the consulting services agreement.

Strategic initiatives. A brief listing of the various specific initiatives of the project, in summary format. Here are a few examples:

- Change our marketing position from "excellent local vendor" to "boutique national firm."
- Change the emphasis of our sales efforts from new client acquisition to existing account penetration through cross-selling, upselling, and personalized account management.
- Increase the rigor of our hiring process and put consistent employee-selection criteria in place across all departments in all business units.
- Enhance our research and development capability with a structured program for developing ideas for new products, services, processes, and patents.
- Build more strategic alliances and partnerships with important firms and industries related to our core business.
- Increase the diversity of our workforce with expanded programs to recruit, retain, and promote minority employees, managers, and senior executives.

Accomplishments to date. A more detailed listing of what has been accomplished up to this point in the project, and where those pieces fit into the overall plan outlined in the first two sections. An example is provided below:

> This report describes our accomplishments over the past nine months in implementing the strategic initiatives and the action steps in that plan. In summary, the company has made substantial progress in completing the initiatives identified in the plan. Of the 19 action steps listed, we have totally or partially completed 13 items, including:
>
> - the strengthening of our research environment
> - the introduction of the Jump Start diversity program
> - the creation of a new Alliance Partnership Center in the Houston office

Chapter 4: Evaluating Outcomes and Making Adjustments

Action items in progress. A more detailed item-by-item listing of the various project components and their status, using categories such as Ongoing, Started, Partially Completed, Final Stage, Completed, and To Be Started.

Note: This section is really the heart of the progress report, communicating "where we are today." An example is provided below:

> **Action item:** Start a minority recruiting and retention program ("Jump Start") to increase the number of minority employees, managers, and senior executives
>
> **Status: Completed.** In February of 2006, the company announced the creation of Jump Start, a partnership program with four leading graduate schools and four external executive-search firms to expand the diversity of our workforce and the managerial ranks of our business units. Jump Start targets highly qualified recent graduates and experienced professionals. While the Jump Start program is open to candidates from any background, the hope is that the program will encourage more high-quality candidates from under-represented backgrounds to pursue a career with our organization. During the Spring of 2006, we will be recruiting our first group of candidates from this program.

What's left to be done. This section contains a broad overview of the project elements that lie ahead and includes estimated time frames and summaries.

(Name of Project)
Progress Report

Introduction/Vision:
_____
_____

Strategic Initiatives:
_____
_____

Accomplishments to Date:
This report describes our accomplishments over the past ___ months in implementing the strategic initiatives and the action steps in that plan. In summary, the company has made substantial progress in completing the initiatives identified in the plan. Of the ___ action steps listed, we have totally or partially completed ___ items, including:
_____
_____

Action items in progress:

Action item: _____

Status: _____ (Started, Ongoing, Partially Completed, Final Stage, Completed, To Be Started)

Action item: _____

Status: _____ (Started, Ongoing, Partially Completed, Final Stage, Completed, To Be Started)

Action item: _____

Status: _____ (Started, Ongoing, Partially Completed, Final Stage, Completed, To Be Started)

What's left to be done:
_____
_____

The Fine Art of "Clienting"

There are about a zillion books on consulting, and none that I could find on "clienting." It goes without saying that the quality and quantity of attention that a consultant receives from you, the "client" manager, will likely make or break the success of the relationship, as well as the business outcomes of the engagement.

So here is my small contribution to the narrow field of clienting: a few basic words of advice to solidify and strengthen the relationship between you and the consultant you have hired.

Be open. As a manager, you must be frank and forthcoming about the problems that face your organization. Tell your consultant the entire story: the good, the bad, and the ugly. This is no time to be shy, hold back, or sugar-coat the truth. You've asked for a full solution, and that's difficult to get when you only reveal half the problem!

Follow through. Sooner or later (sooner, if you've hired a consultant worth her salt), your people will need to get into action. Make sure you don't make commitments to act unless you can keep them. Remember, the manager-consultant relationship is supposed to be one of collaboration. Your consultant wants to do it *with* you, not *to* you. You must hold up your end of that bargain. Failure to deliver on a commitment made to a consultant should be considered the same as failure to deliver on a commitment made to the organization. Why? Because it is the same thing.

Communicate. Keep the channels open. Be willing to share new information as it relates to the consultant's tasks. Connect the consultant to people who can accelerate the work. Lubricate the communications process: Invite the consultant to relevant meetings, conference calls, and client meetings. Show, rather than tell. The more open and frequent the communication with all stakeholders, the less mystery, suspicion, and rumor mongering the consultant will have to deal with as he tries to get his work done on your behalf.

Walk the talk. If your consultant is working on a customer service initiative and one of the service standards you're implementing involves call response time, you need to lead the way internally. If you've decided a customer service rep should answer the phone within two rings, you should answer *your* phone within two rings, even if you only deal with internal calls and internal customers. Consistency and leading by example are two of the most powerful tools you have at your disposal to make sure the changes you're asking others to make will, in fact, stick (and stick long after the consultants have left the building).

Change Management 101

As a manager, your work with your consultant will probably involve change. And change is always an emotionally charged issue. Whatever its magnitude, only you, the manager, can decide whether or not implementing these changes is appropriate, useful, and valuable. Once you decide to go ahead with the changes, trust your judgment, your people, and your consultant enough to make those changes stick.

Change is instantaneous—it's the transition that's hard. Transition is done in three steps:

1. Let go of the current reality.
2. Proceed as the way becomes clear (perhaps awkwardly and reluctantly at first).
3. Adapt to the new reality on the way to realizing the future vision.

The big myth behind all the management and leadership thinking around change is that change is good. There are really two parts to debunking this myth:

Chapter 4: Evaluating Outcomes and Making Adjustments

1. Change is neither good nor bad: It's simply inevitable.
2. Human nature makes people dislike change, and being a cheerleader for change will make people dislike *you*.

So as the manager in charge of leading this change, what are you supposed to do? First of all, I would strongly discourage managers from ever offering something as ridiculous as a "change" workshop. That's like doing a workshop on root canal and expecting applause and appreciation afterward. People will hate you, hate your consultant, and perhaps even start to hate the organization, and some will do their utmost to undermine you and the initiative you are championing—not a good situation.

In fact, this is the worst kind of set-up that you can subject yourself and your consulting resources to, wittingly or not.

Never abdicate your leadership responsibilities by hiring an outside consultant, speaker, trainer, author, or management guru to come in and tell people to stop whining, move their "cheese," or do whatever is in the current "flavor of the month" change book or seminar.

A wise manager or consultant always deals in specifics, not generalizations. What is the change that you are trying to implement and manage? New organizational structure? New technology? New responsibilities? Merger or acquisition? New leadership? New compensation structure? Determine the specifics, and you will be in a position to best determine how to get your desired result. (And it's fine if that result is getting people to stop whining—it just has to be articulated openly!)

In short, you and your consultant will become evangelists for the specific new outcomes and results for your organization and for your people, but you will not be wasting your time trying to engender warm, fuzzy emotions for the change itself or for change in general.

To get back to my earlier analogy, paint a very clear picture of clean, strong, healthy teeth and the ability to eat any food you like, and don't try to convince people how wonderful a root canal procedure can be.

What to Do if Conflict Arises

Conflict is a natural part of human relations. We experience conflict in our personal and our professional lives, and not all conflict is bad. However, when conflict arises between you and your consultant, things can get ugly fast. So let me share with you some specific conflict-management skills that will stand you in good stead when working with your consultant and anyone else in your professional life.

Step 1: Deal effectively with anger. You can't resolve a conflict and find a good solution if you and/or the other person are too angry to think straight, or you fail to acknowledge your feelings.

Step 2: Do your homework. Think before you act. Ask yourself the following questions to prepare for the resolution process:

- How does this conflict affect us?
- What interests or values are at stake for each of us?
- What prejudices or assumptions do we each have about the other?
- What approaches or style would be best here?
- If I want to collaborate, what is the right time and place to initiate that?

Step 3: Set a positive tone. Invite the other person to help resolve the conflict. ("Could we talk?") State positive intentions. ("I'd like to make things better between us.") Acknowledge and validate the other person. ("I can see this is difficult for you, too.

Thank you for working with me on this.") Show appreciation and respect. ("You've done a fabulous job on the project, and we wouldn't be where we are today without you. I just wanted to address some specific concerns. . . .")

Step 4: Use ground rules. Examples:

- One person talks at a time.
- Discuss behavior, not personalities.
- Discuss specifics, not generalities.
- Focus exclusively on the issue at hand. Don't raise other problems, past history, etc.
- Work to improve the situation.
- Stay calm.

Step 5: Discuss and define the problem. One at a time, each person shares issues and feelings. Use effective listening and speaking techniques. Identify interests and needs. If necessary, discuss assumptions, suspicions, and values. Summarize new understandings.

Step 6: Brainstorm possible solutions. Each person contributes ideas to satisfy interests and needs. Don't criticize or evaluate ideas yet. Be creative. (Use "I can . . ." or "We could . . ." rather than "You should . . ." or "You'd better. . . .")

Step 7: Evaluate and choose solutions. Solutions should be:

- Mutually agreeable
- Realistic
- Specific
- Balanced

Solutions should address the main interests of both parties.

Step 8: Follow up. Check back with each other at an agreed-on time and date. If the agreement isn't working, use the same process to revise it.

Are We There Yet? Wrapping up the Work

The reason that client companies sometimes end up with a "shadow workforce" of on-site consultants who are there for years and years is that nobody defined the end point of the work at the outset. Worse yet, there may actually *be* no end point, because the company has essentially *hired* (not engaged) consultants rather than employees. It's my belief that long-term consulting shouldn't be called *consulting.* It should go by its real name, which is *boutique hiring*.

This brings us to a very important question: Are we there yet?

Like most things that come at the successful end of a project, the answer to this question needs to be thought out at the beginning: Are you clear about the purpose of your consultant's work assignment? Again, let simplicity be your guide, and ask the following questions early on:

- If we have to leave some things undone, which things am I willing to let go? And why?
- How are we currently measuring our success in this area? What do those numbers show?
- How much improvement would I like to see, and in what time frame?
- Who else is impacted by this project? What do they think the endpoint should be?
- How will I know when we're done?

Chapter 4: Evaluating Outcomes and Making Adjustments

- What metrics will I be looking at to measure the effectiveness of this initiative?
- When will "the needle start to move" in response to the changes made thus far?
- Is there a time lag or delay between implementation and measurable results?
- Even if we're not "there" yet, would this be a good time to take a break from the consulting work and evaluate before moving on to solve the next piece of the puzzle?

> This is not the end—it is not even the beginning of the end—but it is perhaps the end of the beginning.
> —*Winston Churchill,* Victory in Egypt speech, November 10, 1942

When you closed a significant chapter of your professional life managing a consulting project that has been both challenging and rewarding, you are sure that you have everything wrapped up. You are so confident that when your consultant suggests that you jointly run a "closure" workshop, you politely decline and reassure him or her that you can "take it from here." After all, the project is done, so now everyone can finally take some richly deserved vacation time, right?

Whoa! Resist this temptation to ignore the closure process, because this is precisely when the learning takes place, the value is realized, and hidden problems are identified.

The closure process is a time when you and your organization need to look back and learn to ensure that the outcome has been delivered and that learning has been transferred along the way. Both will have a profound impact on the sustainability of the consulting project.

It is also important for the consultant. After all, collaborative consulting is founded on the principle of sustainable change—not simply short-lived satisfaction. Your consultant must work to ensure that you, the client, are able to fly solo before he disengages and moves on. In fact, no consultant worth his salt closes out a project until he is sure it can be sustained.

Chapter 5
Consultant as Change Agent, Advocate, and Mentor

Most consultants are expected to play several roles, including change agent, advocate, and mentor. Every consultant, however, is responsible for creating value above and beyond the "terms and conditions" of their consulting agreement. It's up to you, as the manager, to get the most value you can from your consultant and to make sure that the consulting expertise doesn't leave the building at the end of the project, but rather is transferred inside your organization in meaningful and lasting ways.

What Every Consultant Should Provide

Steve Jobs said, "Creativity is just having enough dots to connect... connect experiences and synthesize new things." Of course, a consultant should provide clear and actionable solutions to your immediate problems and challenges. But as a manager, you also need to extract all the "cross-pollination" value from your consultants as well. Ask them to connect the dots and work with both their vertical expertise and horizontal knowledge.

A handful of examples:

- If you work for an airline and your challenge is to clean and turn around planes in less time, connect the dots and do what a NASCAR pit crew does to turn a car around in a matter of seconds.

- If you work for a hospital system and your challenge is to streamline the admitting process and reduce backlogs and wait time, connect the dots and find out how industry-leading hotel chains optimize their check-in processes.
- If you work for a non-profit employment center and your challenge is to get welfare-to-work candidates to show up for job interviews, connect the dots and do what dental offices do: phone the next day's patients to remind them of their appointments.

So how can you do more of this? It's easier, cheaper (heck, it's often free!), and more valuable than you can imagine.

Consulting colleagues of mine agreed to help a leading men's retail clothing chain increase their sales. Their "connect the dots" experience: to spend an hour at a local shopping center, pretending they were aliens from another planet. The consultant wanted them to observe how humans moved about their environment. What attracted them to stop and pick things up? How were things arranged? What traffic patterns were in place at a shoe store, women's boutique, music store, natural food store, vitamin shop, pet store, etc.?

This simple connect-the-dots exercise, helped the retail client monetize the potential increase in sales across hundreds of their stores, and the result was in the millions of dollars. From an hour at the mall!

That's what I mean by connect the dots.

> ### Ways to Connect More Dots
>
> Get out from behind your desk and circulate.
>
> Take field trips and visit odd places.
>
> Read magazines you've never seen before.
>
> Go to trade shows for different industries.
>
> Look at your personal hobbies and make connections.
>
> Keep a "crazy idea" journal and fill it.
>
> Visit museums, libraries, and stores, and go in to "absorb" mode.
>
> Develop your sense of curiosity, and ask "dumb" questions.
>
> Look for patterns and similarities in unlikely places.
>
> Develop your sense of analogy. Start asking *What is this like?*
>
> Listen to different kinds of music and talk radio programs. Sample new TV programs.
>
> Pick up collections of quotations and browse through them.
>
> Ask your kids for answers.

Maximizing Consulting Value

In the consulting world, time is not money—time is time. *Value* is money. Let me explain several kinds of value so that we can assign some specific behaviors to that mysterious word.

Data value. Information, data, and research that consultants create, find, or share that connect directly with the business challenge you are working to solve. (Or another challenge that is important to your organization but is unrelated to the project immediately at hand. Imagine that!)

Experience value. The skills, tools, background, and expertise that your consultant has developed over the years that can be directly applied to your current situation, but that otherwise would be very difficult to develop internally. For example, master computer criminals who become computer security consultants bring experience value to their employers. Would you spend time and money training your IT folks to rob banks or steal identities? Of course not. But you'd want to hire someone with that experience, wouldn't you?

Convenience value. Access, ease of use, and flexibility are examples of convenience value. For example, if you have a consultant in your local city, he or she might offer you on-demand service with access to them on weekends or on off-hours, or make you a priority on their calendar. If you value the notion of "anytime access" versus "billing for access," the focus shifts to getting your organization to your destination, not on running the meter for every phone call, meeting, or work session.

Connection value. Your consultant's network, their business contacts, and any additional services available from a single source (your consultant) are examples of connection value. Good consultants are *aggregators* of expertise. Would it impress you if you ask your diversity consultant for a good Web designer and she gives you a name *and* offers to arrange a meeting and invites your IT manager to boot?

Scouting value. New ideas, cross-pollination, and keeping her radar scope tuned to a broad spectrum of developments in related and unrelated fields put your consultant in a very strong position to offer you solutions that no one else can. After all, the last thing your shoe company needs is someone who knows shoes inside and out. Your organization is already full of those people!

But what could your shoe company learn from someone who loves going to Las Vegas or works on weekends fixing boats or lives on a farm or flies antique planes or reads books on quantum physics or is married to a film producer or has a degree in zoology or happens to be up on the latest methods of connecting people through technology such as *VOIP* or *IM* or *blogging* or *advertainment?*

Make Sure You're Learning to Fish

There's an old Chinese proverb that says, "Give a man a fish and you feed him for a day. Teach a man to fish and you feed him for a lifetime." Well, good consulting involves a lot of teaching and a lot of learning. And as a leader, you have access to a great source of learning: your consultant. Not every consultant is a great teacher, but the good ones truly are. Every manager should be a learner, but must also make sure that others are learning too.

But never think of this learning as learning for its own sake. Take what you've learned from your consultant and apply it, modify it, expand it, develop it, share it, teach others, and boil it down to its essence in real, concrete business terms that you can use in your immediate environment. Then focus like a laser beam on application, application, application! Learn from every source, think, and then translate that learning into appropriate, useful, meaningful action.

The Consulting Project Clinic

One way to apply new learning during a consulting project is to hold project clinics. To get maximum value from your external consultants, the organization should only have to ask them each question *once.* Project clinics help you gather the answers to your questions and communicate those answers throughout your organization.

Here's what I mean: Whenever an organization does not possess a required skill, it should buy the services of an appropriate external consultant. The consultant will work with you to answer your questions and help you to make effective use of a product, process, tool, or technique. The next time you have questions, the consultant returns and you go through the same cycle: The questions are answered, you make progress, and everyone is happy.

This use of external consultants is an effective investment only if you are using them to answer *new* questions. But if you are continually using external consultants to solve the same problems, it is a sign that your organization is not learning—clearly, you need to develop some mechanism for trapping and transferring knowledge. Consultancy is a product, and like any other product, it can be made visible, tangible, and transferable. In order to take full advantage of external consulting resources, an organization needs a procedure for capturing and communicating answers. What has been learned from the consultant?

The project clinic is an alternative to advanced training; instead of taking additional courses, the project clinic provides "on the job" training. The aim of a project clinic is to keep a project healthy—healthy in the sense that tools and techniques are being effectively used to assist the project team to build the system. Hospitals are places where people go when they are sick and need to be cured. Clinics exist to keep people healthy. When people go to a clinic, they are taking preventive measures to make sure that they stay healthy and are kept aware of developments in healthcare techniques.

Project clinics do the same thing for consulting projects. The clinic is designed to make sure that the project stays healthy by identifying and solving problems and ensuring that the project continues to make satisfactory progress.

Chapter 5: Consultant as Change Agent, Advocate, and Mentor

The clinic is a mixture of formal lectures, informal discussions, and work sessions. The subject of the clinic is driven by the current needs of the project. To give you an idea of how varied these clinics can be, here are some examples of subjects from various consulting clinics:

- To get the project started (a kickoff clinic)
- To verify the context of a technical system
- To explain how to model an event response
- To quickly create audio or video tutorials using in-house equipment
- To show new methods of interacting with customers
- To review the estimates for a project
- To draft communication documents and bullet scripts for managers to use with staff
- To define the interfaces between multiple projects
- To design and implement sample transactions
- To hold a tutoring session on effective meeting skills
- To demo and debrief a new product, process, or service prototype
- To plan a management presentation using the projects' models
- To co-create and refine marketing and sales collateral materials
- To meet with subject matter experts for "master" classes and executive briefings
- To inform managers about measurable deliverables
- To build templates for future distribution and re-use

In short, the project clinic is a hands-on workshop using material from the real project. The motto is "learn as you go." All team members come away with a greater sense of involvement, ownership, and engagement with the consultants and the project

The Manager's Pocket Guide to Using Consultants

outcome itself. (In fact, project team members, not your consultants, might be the best people to lead certain clinics.)

Another option is to select several employees to take the training to become internal consultants. The training consists of attendance at all of the project clinics, special technical sessions, and "train the trainer" sessions on how to do knowledge transfer. By the end of the project, you want each internal consultant to be able to run his or her own project clinics, thus spreading the knowledge and application capability even further within your organization.

Knowledge Transfer and Tracking

Check those activities and clinics that will make your projects more successful.

Activities

❑ Team meeting	❑ E-learning
❑ Consultant meeting	❑ Self-study materials
❑ Seminar	❑ Audio or video tutorial
❑ Hands-on training	❑ Peer group meeting

Project Clinics

❑ Kickoff	❑ Sales
❑ Technical information	❑ Customer Service
❑ Communications	❑ Executive briefing
❑ Sample transaction	❑ Demo and debrief
❑ Master class with SME	❑ Measurement and reporting
❑ Template and document building	❑ Tutoring session

Audience

❑ Senior leadership	❑ Technical staff
❑ Front-line staff	❑ Customer service
❑ Sales	❑ Marketing
❑ Research and Development	❑ Operations
❑ Customers/Clients	❑ Other:

Chapter 5: Consultant as Change Agent, Advocate, and Mentor

What a Consultant Can Do That You Can't

Often, a consultant's value is pretty basic: As an outsider, he or she can see things, hear things, and say things that the manager simply cannot see, hear, or say. Here's what I mean: As a manager, you've probably repeatedly pointed out to people in the organization that a certain process or system is flawed or broken, but no one seems to take it seriously. However, a consultant coming in from the outside can take one look, do a bit of research, and report his conclusion that the process or system is flawed or broken, and BINGO: The emperor suddenly realizes that he is, indeed, wearing no clothes. It's an amazing effect, and one I'm sure you've seen in action many times.

A consultant's "outsider" status can be very valuable and helpful to you as a manager. Consider your consultant a catalyst for the action you want to see—and an ally in the process of implementing it. In this case, the "politics" of the situation work in your favor.

Politics can also present the manager with an opportunity to become manipulative. Here are two times when bringing in a consultant becomes a very detrimental and expensive form of playing politics:

1. When you're asking the consultant to deliver a message that **you're afraid to deliver yourself.** Example: The manager rounds up people who are unknowingly about to be laid off and asks a consultant to come in and deliver a *Who Moved My Cheese*-type seminar.
2. When you're intentionally "front-loading" and asking the consultant to deliver a message that **you've delivered a thousand times before** (such as bringing in an HR IT consultant to "report" that your company is in desperate need of some HR software that you want—software that, say, the CEO has repeatedly refused to implement).

The two scenarios above are only examples, but you get the idea. It's not fair to you or to your consultant for you to hide behind or try to manipulate their "outsider" status. In fact, consultants who take their profession and their ethics seriously will refuse to work under conditions such as these. Consider that a mark in the plus column, and when your next legitimate consulting need arises, call these folks first!

Maximizing the Value of an Outside-Insider

My own consulting experience and that of colleagues has allowed me to observe a wide array of consulting relationships. Here are a handful of "Next Practices" for managing and maximizing the value of consultants.

Get the Most out of Your Consultants!
Next Practices

✓ Once a consultant is in the building, consider yourself a *peer consultant*—not a boss, not an employee, not even a manager. Co-create the conditions for project success. *Hint:* You'll build your own consulting skills in the process!

✓ Establish clear expectations for both sides at the beginning of a project. This is crucial to the project's ultimate success. Document as much as you can, and make sure to design the information flow for maximum openness at every step.

✓ Set up an initial meeting with the consultant and any steering or advisory committee members (if appropriate). Senior management staff as a rule do *not* like surprises. Involve and engage them on whatever level is appropriate so that they have a sense of the nature and purpose of the project (and a sense of ownership of the outcomes).

✓ Review scope, objectives, work plan, and time lines—*frequently*.

(continued)

Chapter 5: Consultant as Change Agent, Advocate, and Mentor

Get the Most out of Your Consultants!
Next Practices *(concluded)*

✓ Set up a two-way communication plan with your consultant and other key stakeholders for the life of the project. You need a feedback process for sharing updates, questions, newly uncovered information, or technical data with your consultant.

✓ Sign a formal contract that clearly spells out exactly what is expected. If your consultant is smart and does NOT bill by the hour, day, or week, also experiment with putting a bonus structure in place for early completion.

✓ Review final products to ensure that they are consistent with your requirements and agreed-upon expectations.

✓ Make sure that all contributors are publicly recognized and personally thanked for their role in the project's ultimate outcome (not just at the end of the project, but also as new data and results come in and new milestones are achieved that stemmed from the original work).

✓ Debrief consultants and stakeholders, and assess the outcomes in hard dollars and cents, percentages, or other metrics that are important to you. You'll look brilliant, and the consultant will have a clearly documented success on her track record.

Chapter 6
Consulting Dangers, Pitfalls, and Traps

If there were such a thing as the "Professional Joke Olympics," lawyers would win gold and consultants would win silver. Why is consulting the #2 most jibed-at profession? Because of the many dangers, pitfalls, and traps that clients can fall victim to. However, with some forethought, preparation, and goodwill, you can avoid or work through many of these potential dangers. In this chapter, we'll look at how to avoid making mistakes when using a consultant.

Don't Accept "Cookie-Cutter" Work

Several large consulting companies have been publicly exposed over the past few years for their sloppy practices—for "working" over a period of months on a client problem, and then handing in an impressive-looking final report (for which they collected hefty fees) that turned out to be a word-for-word copy of something they prepared for somebody else on the same issue. It seems that in some cases, staff members forgot to change the names on all the pages! The consulting firms wound up with egg on their faces and with lawsuits. Wouldn't it be better for the client (and far more interesting for the consultants) to look at the unique angles to each engagement and to come to each set of problems with a fresh perspective and very few pre-conceived notions? To actually improve the flesh-and-blood situation, rather than copy-and-paste another 300-page report?

How many meetings have you attended where you had an overwhelming sense of deja-vu? The same people making the same suggestions to solve the same problems in the same ways. Do no accept the "same-o lame-o" solutions from a consultant; many firms use "cookie cutter" methods and proprietary tools and approaches (Problem #422 requires Intervention #422). A smarter approach is to use specific methodologies that are customized to your own situation and organization, and that are based on your objectives, your context, and what your people are ready to implement. A solution that you and your consultant collaborate on is going to lead to project success with far greater certainty than having the consultant pick out something from a book. "Off the shelf" surveys, models, matrices and other proprietary formulas can force you into a pre-set "client mold." Your situation is unique, and you deserve a unique and custom approach that your consultant should create based on sound and proven principles, not on pre-fabricated solutions. Do not accept anything that looks like a templatized report or tool just because it has your organization's name on it.

Beware of Arrogance (on Both Sides of the Table)

I hate arrogance. I hate it in clients and I also hate it in other consultants. Strictly speaking, the dictionary definition of arrogance is "Overbearing self-worth or self-importance, marked by a feeling or assumption of one's superiority toward others." Who needs that?

The good news is that if you've decided to hire a consultant, chances are excellent that you're not arrogant. After all, successful and wealthy individuals hire financial advisors; successful professional golfers hire coaches; and successful managers and companies hire consultants. Yes, you can achieve the same results without consultants, but with consultants you can

Chapter 6: Consulting Dangers, Pitfalls, and Traps

achieve more, more quickly and with more certainty. Truly excellent companies such as Hewlett Packard or IBM do not hire consultants because they believe they are weak—they hire consultants because they want to remain strong, and do not want to waste their precious time and money on learning what someone else has already learned and can teach them.

The bad news is that clients who need consulting help the most (and who could most benefit from outside expertise) will never call for help. Why? Because of their arrogance! They don't need consultants and their feeble little services. Ha! They're MEGACORP and they've just had their best year ever. Profits and productivity are way up; the stock price is up; they're winning awards left and right. Yup, they've got nothing left to learn from anybody. They're at the top of their game. Tick, tick, tick, tick . . .

I once met with the leaders of a large financial services firm in suburban Philadelphia. Over lunch, one of the senior managers asked me to talk more about the issue of arrogance and its frequent companion, complacency, because she thought they might be experiencing these things as they introduced new financial products. The company's leaders would set goals, reach them, and then sit back and congratulate themselves on a job well done. The concept of stretching further, sometimes a lot further, was not in their mindset. They were happy with incremental growth, because after all, it was still growth—and who can argue with that?

Sometimes the biggest challenge people have in working for an already very successful organization is replacing top performers' complacency with commitment to do better still. Why don't people inside successful organizations naturally commit to always doing better? The prevailing mindset might very well be "Don't mess with success," and to a certain extent, that is good advice. Bear in mind the wisdom of Hippocrates who outlined to physicians the following responsibilities:

> Declare the past, diagnose the present, foretell the future. As to diseases, make a habit of two things—to help, or at least to do no harm.

So the last piece of that advice ("do no harm") equates to "don't mess with success" or "if it ain't broke, don't fix it."

The point to consider, however, is how to reach for the next level of success without doing harm to the status quo. Common sense suggests that it's impossible, and it is. After all, the word *breakthrough* does contain the word *break*—as in, "if it ain't broke, break it!" But arrogant leaders and arrogant organizations are very reluctant to break what's working in order to replace it with something untried that might work much better.

Changing the game is not an incremental process. Blowing away the competition is not an incremental process. Revolutionizing customer experiences is not an incremental process.

Sustainable business success and arrogance simply don't mix.

Put Expertise above Experience

A lot of consultants have built their reputation by specializing in one industry or type of client. This can be problematic, however: If I'm GM and I hire you, how do I know that you won't bring the same set of answers and strategies to Ford next month? And how do I know your thinking is fresh, and not calcified or frozen in time from your last original thought in 1977?

Let's say you have a choice between two consultants. Consultant A has a lot of experience and a solid track record in your industry (we'll stick with the auto industry for a moment—pretend you

Chapter 6: Consulting Dangers, Pitfalls, and Traps

work for BMW). Consultant B has done a lot of different kinds of work for clients in many industries: Disney, AOL, Sara Lee, Toyota, Microsoft, and JP Morgan Chase. Quick—who would you hire?

When I ask this question in my seminars, about 80 percent of the audience chooses Consultant A, and only about 20 percent chooses Consultant B. The amazing thing is that if you choose Consultant B, you'd be getting so much more value—the value of *expertise* over *experience!* Consultant B brings expertise and ideas from past projects and other firms and industries. Hiring her would boost your source of fresh, novel, valuable ideas. This "cross pollination" is a bullet-proof method for tapping into almost unlimited brain-power that could never exist in any one industry or market segment. Do you want a consultant who's been working on a wide variety of issues, who can help you cross-pollinate? Or do you want someone whose scope is just as narrow as your current challenge? Think carefully before you decide.

In his brilliant book *Jump Start Your Business Brain*, Doug Hall writes, "Feed your brain with multisensory stimuli that are both related and unrelated to your challenge. The greater the diversity of opinions and perspectives you gather, the more effective you will be in creating ideas that can truly grow your business."

In other words, cross-pollinate. Ideas are all around you. It's your job to absorb, recombine, and apply them. And, of course, the same goes for any consultant worth her salt—broad experience across many industries opens up a whole world of ideas. As one of my clients so eloquently put it, "There are no real new ideas; the wheel, fire, religion, yelling, and sliced bread have already been discovered, and all subsequent ideas spawned from those. The real value lies in taking old ideas, updating them, combining them, and creating new value from them."

In my seminars, I sometimes ask the group what they can learn from businesses very different from their own. It opens their eyes to new practices (frequent flyer miles, packaging, subscriptions, bundling, super-sizing) that are commonplace in other contexts, but rather revolutionary in their world. Try it the next time you're stuck.

Accountability for Results Starts with You

The word *accountability* is freely bandied about in the business world, so let me nail it down in fairly simple terms:

> Accountability is the connection between intention and action—it connects what you say you'll do to what actually gets done. It brings structure, focus, and clarity to business relationships. It is your promise and obligation to yourself and to the people around you to deliver specific, defined results. People who are accountable are aware of and are willing to live with the positive and negative consequences of their actions and inactions. If they want different consequences, they take different actions.

Accountability for results starts with accountability for accountability!

John G. Miller has written a fabulous book called *QBQ! The Question Behind the Question.* In it, he explores the root cause of questions such as these:

- Why do we have to go through all this change?
- Who dropped the ball?
- Why can't they communicate better?
- When is that department going to do its job right?
- When am I going to find good people?
- Why don't they share the vision?
- Who's going to clarify my job?

Chapter 6: Consulting Dangers, Pitfalls, and Traps

He suggests that these questions wouldn't be asked if there was personal accountability. Sadly, lack of accountability is rampant inside even small three-person organizations, and it is worse inside larger organizations, where it has that much more space to expand. Lack of accountability is extremely dangerous for a manager. Let me explain: How many times have you engaged a consultant and then sat back as they did their work, while you filled the role of observer? That's not collaboration—that's treating management as a spectator sport.

Here's a quiz, again courtesy of John G. Miller. See if you can complete the following sentences. I'll start you off:

A poor sailor blames <u>the wind.</u>

A poor teacher blames the _____.

A poor salesperson blames the _____.

A poor parent blames the _____.

A poor manager blames the _____.

A poor employee blames the _____.

A poor consultant blames the _____.

Blame is a symptom of a lack of accountability. No matter where you are in an organization, the buck stops with *you.* In my seminars, I'll often ask people, "Who does a *good* consultant blame?" Most people answer, "Themselves." The correct answer is *no one*. A good consultant is "blame-less" in that he does not believe that blaming is productive. A good consultant *acts* to fix the situation.

The next time you sense a lack of accountability either inside your own organization or while working with a consulting team, head the problem off at the pass and start with an accountability roundtable for all the key players in the organization. That's real win-win, and it will raise the bar for everyone's performance, engagement, and commitment to the desired outcomes.

Ask yourself the following questions:

> **Accountability Questions**
>
> How can I manage this project more effectively?
>
> How can I participate more fully in the success of this project?
>
> How can I contribute more to the project's outcomes?
>
> How can I make sure knowledge transfer happens continuously?
>
> How can I facilitate my consultant's success?
>
> How can I better support my team during this transition period?
>
> How can I better (more quickly, more cheaply) implement my consultant's recommendations?
>
> What can I do to make this project's outcomes more lasting and meaningful?
>
> What knowledge and skills can I contribute?
>
> What training and resources can I provide my team to make this learning stick?
>
> What do I need to do to maintain and increase executive buy-in to this project?
>
> What results do I need to measure to "take the temperature" of the project?
>
> What do I need to do to tie the success of this project directly into one (or more) of our strategic initiatives and long-range goals?
>
> Whose support do I need for this project if we are to be successful?
>
> What follow-up activities, tools, and strategies will keep us moving forward after the project is officially over?

Advice-Based Consulting vs. Product-Based Consulting

There are two fundamental types of consulting: advice-based and product-based. It's important to understand the difference between the two, since crossed wires in this area are often a source of consulting confusion and client disappointment.

Chapter 6: Consulting Dangers, Pitfalls, and Traps

Advice-based consulting is a business relationship where value is exchanged by way of information, advice, and knowledge, all delivered from a strategic vantage point. The operational phrase for the consultant is *I know*. This is the traditional consultant-as-expert model, where the consultant comes in, studies the situation, creates a detailed report, and plops a big binder on your desk. Implementation is strictly up to you.

The big binder simply gets moved to the CEO's bookshelf and the organization continues with business as usual. In his book *Process Consultation*, Dr. Edgar Schein, consulting expert and professor at the Sloan School of Management at MIT, writes that over 90 percent of consulting projects never get implemented.

Product-based consulting is a term I use for creating tangibles or "deliverables": employee training manuals, operational handbooks, technology rollout plans, sales collateral materials, Web sites, client presentations, seminars, marketing events, HR and legal policy documents, PR plans, and so forth. These are all delivered from a tactical vantage point. The operational phrase for the consultant is *"I do."* Try not to confuse the two types of consulting. You can't afford to contract for one when what you really need is the other or contract for only one when you need both. Let's say a consulting firm is brought in soon after the merger of two companies for what seems like a simple product-based assignment: the CEO is hiring the firm to reconcile the policies and procedures of the two former firms now that they have become one. Naturally, the situation the consultants find themselves immersed in is much more complicated than what the CEO led them to believe. The new organization needs advice-based help far beyond the "product" of some quick revisions to an HR manual. However, a revised manual is all the client asks for.

The opposite situation occurs when a company needs only a small push in one direction or another, and instead contracts for a multi-year, multi-million-dollar project because that's all that their

Fortune 100 consulting firm offers (or that's all they know to ask consultants for). A customized six-month leadership training program for in-house use (a product) would probably have done the trick, but a large consulting firm manages to convince the key buyers inside the client organization that to solve their problem, they really need to build a four-tier, 20-course corporate university and in-house "School of Leadership." This solution, of course, is a perfect example of the "killing a fly with an elephant gun" syndrome that many consulting firms have become famous for.

Be aware of the difference between advice-based consulting and product-based consulting. And remember the old saying, "Be careful what you ask for—you might just get it."

Chapter 7
Evaluating Your Consultant's Toolkit

How do you know if you're working with a good consultant or a *great* consultant? Often you don't—until it's too late. However, like working with a craftsman, there are signs at the beginning, the middle, and the end of the work that tell you whether or not you're dealing with a true consulting professional. We'll explore these in this chapter.

Ten Great Questions Your Consultant Should Ask You

Your consultant should have a good idea what is important to you and the organization, and what the organization has done to learn from its mistakes and make itself stronger, smarter, and more competitive. He or she should ask you questions like these:

1. What are you passionate about?
2. Are you being too cautious?
3. What is your dream for this organization?
4. How can I help you?
5. What five things can we do right now?
6. What have you learned from your success?
7. So what?
8. What's the dumbest thing you could do?
9. Did today matter?
10. How will we know when we're done?

1. **What are you passionate about?** Neil Simon once defined the word *talent* as ". . . the gift PLUS the passion—a desire to succeed so intense that no force on earth can stop it." If your consultant finds out what you are personally passionate about and then finds out what your organization's senior and front-line leadership people are passionate about, then she will know a lot about your company's priorities, values, goals, and motivators.

2. **Are you being too cautious?** Sometimes clients call consultants when they know what they need to do but are afraid to make the leap on their own. Andy Grove, CEO of Intel, said, "There is at least one point in the history of any company when you have to change dramatically to rise to the next level of performance. Miss that moment, and you start to decline." The overwhelming way most companies "miss that moment" is by being too cautious. A good consultant is willing to play make-believe—to play in the realm of fantasy and what-if and crazy talk.

   Hajime Mitarai—the Japanese industrialist who, as president of Canon, Inc., introduced nonconformist marketing strategies that turned the electronics manufacturer into one of the world's most innovative companies—once said, "We are crazy. We should do something when people say it is 'crazy.' If people say something is 'good,' it means someone else is already doing it."

3. **What is your dream for this organization?** I once sat in a conference room 30 miles west of Philadelphia at a Fortune 500 client's world headquarters. I opened the meeting with this same question. Of the 10 people in the room, three faces lit up momentarily, only to be dimmed seconds later by six blank stares and one pair of rolling eyeballs. (I should have

Chapter 7: Evaluating Your Consultant's Toolkit

asked those three people to stay in the room and had everyone else leave, because the meeting would be a waste of their time. As always, hindsight is 20-20.)

The dreams I heard in that room were quite powerful. People spoke of getting back to basics; of a renewed sense of trust and collaboration; of getting back to the entrepreneurial roots of the company. These dreams were important. These people were willing to spend money on dreams, go to bat for dreams, and make changes for dreams. These are the people your consultants should be talking with.

4. **How can I help you?** This is a very simple, direct question. It almost doesn't matter when your consultant asks it. Its main purpose is to establish his intention to help; its secondary purpose is to gather information that he needs to do his job.

5. **What five things can we do right now?** Asking this question immediately places action on the table—before the needs analyses, before the assessments, before the meetings. It's sort of like having dessert first.

This is not jumping the gun; it's getting 70 percent of the work done in the first meeting! As Ralph Waldo Emerson said, "An ounce of action is worth a ton of theory."

6. **What have you learned from your successes?** It's only common sense to try to learn from your mistakes. Sometimes consultants will go down that path just to review what hasn't worked and perhaps figure out why. There is certainly some value in that, but there's a great deal more value in helping people learn from their successes, and that's what great consultants do. A client might tell you that a successful project or product "just happened" or that "we just got lucky with that one." I don't believe in luck. If you can find

out exactly what was done right, you can help your team consciously replicate what went well and help them become more aware of their strengths.

In my seminars, I ask people to think of a great idea they've had: a successful project, initiative, or work-related experience. I ask them to document their thoughts and emotions before, during, and after that experience. Once that information is captured, we talk about what made that idea or experience "great" and how they can capitalize on the same strengths now, in order to deal with their current challenges.

Of course, the same feelings they put in the "Before" column might be the same feelings they are experiencing right now. If so, the connection and path to a successful outcome are clear, since they're already identifying with Step 1 out of 3. Then we look at the "After" column and I ask the following series of questions:

- What is the greatest thing you can do with these strengths?
- What ideas do you have now about the current situation?
- What is your plan to gain commitment?
- What resources/allies do you need to create this success?

This process lays the blueprint for future success by carefully extracting lessons and tools from past successes.

7. **So what?** A consultant's first responsibility might be to make sure the work he has been hired to do actually *matters*—actually makes a real difference to the company's core business well-being. If it does, great. If it doesn't, that's vital information to bring up early in the process, while there's still time to refocus, revise, and regroup.

Chapter 7: Evaluating Your Consultant's Toolkit

A large consulting firm I worked for decided to create its own proprietary software platform that would integrate all the functionality everyone needed and be fully modular and programmable to accommodate any future needs.

Version 1.0, 2.0, and 3.0 came and went with no release date in sight. There was continual interdepartmental bickering over fundamental aspects of the package, and there were significant bugs in the platform. Meanwhile, business went on just fine: Up-to-date PCs ran all the current applications either through the mainframe or through custom-made PC database programs. After four years of this, the organization fired the entire software development team and its executive leader, after wasting millions of dollars and tens of thousands of people-hours. Nobody asked "So what?"

8. **What's the dumbest thing you could do?** This question is often a great way to create shortcuts to powerful business ideas and solutions. For example, one challenge might be how to create a more powerful marketing message for a high-end law firm.

   Ask "What's the dumbest thing you could do?" in response to this challenge, and you might generate the following "pretty dumb" solutions:

   - Send singing, dancing, juggling clowns to Grand Central Station and have them pass out brochures while wearing sandwich boards bearing the firm's name and logo.

   - Take out a full-page ad in *The Wall Street Journal* and leave it completely blank.

   - Start fax-blasting random lists with slogans like "We're the crookedest lawyers in town. Call us with your problem. With enough cash to grease enough palms, winning your case will be in the bag!"

- Call all the firm's old clients and threaten to release their files to the media if they don't generate at least three referrals in the next 24 hours.

See, now all of these are pretty bad ideas. But they're creative fuel with which a really good idea might reveal itself and take off.

From this, it's a short step to creating an urban, hip campaign aimed at a younger generation of technology, pharmaceutical, or bio-tech companies. Wildly colorful graphics could be mixed with short, meaningful copy to convey the message of integrity, with just the right degree of "coolness" to get attention from this new source of prospective clients.

9. **Did today matter?** Smart consultants must operate along three timelines in order to be successful in the long term, the short term, and the immediate present. In a sense, there should be no such thing as a long-term project: Every project should make an impact today, this week, this month. If it doesn't, how can you say at the end of six months, "Well, we've made a tremendous impact." It's like saying you ate an elephant in one bite. One large bank I know of has the question "Did today matter?" posted on an antique wooden sign over the main entrance, facing in, so that employees see it on their way out the door each day.

10. **How will we know when we're done?** This one is simple—you're done when you have accomplished what you've set out to do.

Debunking the Myths

You've probably heard a lot of things about consultants over the years, good and bad. Before you make decisions about external programs, advice, and services, let's shed a little light on a few of those urban legends.

Chapter 7: Evaluating Your Consultant's Toolkit

Myth #1: You can do more with less. The phrase "do more with less" is insane. Realistically, people can be expected to do one of three things in business:

1. Do less with less.
2. Do more with more (this one's easy).
3. Do less with more.

Let me take a moment to explain the third item, because people sometimes think it's a typo on my slide during a seminar. Doing less with more was a serious problem when there was "more" available (think late 1990s and the dot.com boom times). Hiring more staff, spending more money, buying the latest technology, and having more time often meant that people got careless, sloppy, and slow. Creativity and urgency for action (and sometimes even a basic connection with business realities) left the building when there was always "more" to be thrown at a problem.

Economist E. F. Schumacher said, "Any intelligent fool can make things bigger, more complex, and more violent. It takes a touch of genius—and a lot of courage—to move in the opposite direction." What if you looked for consultants who favored the smaller, the simpler, and the gentler solutions? Winston Churchill was asked how much time he would need to prepare a talk. He replied that his preparation time depended on the talk's duration. When asked about a two-hour speech, he said he could deliver that immediately. When asked about a five-minute speech, he said, "I should need a fortnight to prepare."

The short, simple, direct answers are often the most valuable, and they are the ones that take the most thought and the hardest work.

Myth #2: Consultants are smarter than you. Don't get me wrong—consultants are not going to get rich printing up glossy brochures detailing exactly how dumb they are. But they're also not going to get rich claiming to be smarter than anyone either.

The truth is that the value of a consultant is in direct proportion not to how much *more* they know than you, but how much *different* they know than you. In other words, none of us knows "more" than the other—all we can really do to add value is to learn things outside of our own expertise and to apply that knowledge in useful, relevant, and actionable ways.

A good consultant provides value by doing all these things:

- Listening
- Observing
- Connecting
- Detecting patterns from confusion
- Asking dumb questions
- Paying attention
- Acting with speed, accuracy, and consistency for your business improvement

Myth #3: Time is money. Consultants who bill by the hour or day or week or month are selling themselves short, and selling their clients short as well. In the consulting world, time is time. In the consulting world, *value* is money. If you have a painful toothache and a skilled dentist can solve that problem for $350, would you rather he take two hours to do it with you in the chair, or two minutes? If he solved your problem in two minutes, would you complain of his exorbitant hourly rate? Probably not. Speed has its own inherent value, and so does solving a critical business problem quickly and elegantly, rather than in a long, protracted, painful process.

Myth #4: Information is valuable. This isn't completely a myth. Some clients do value the information they receive from consultants quite a lot, but that's only one piece of the puzzle. William Pollard had this to say about information:

Chapter 7: Evaluating Your Consultant's Toolkit

> Information is a source of learning. But unless it is organized, processed, and available to the right people in a format for decision making, it is a burden, not a benefit.

Clients look to consultants to provide one or more of the following:

Information. Web sites, articles, journals, conference presentations, white papers, research reports, etc.: if you value it, ask your consultant to provide it to you.

Relationship. You, as a manager, might value a deep relationship with your consultant, thinking of this person as a mentor, connector, coach, and catalyst for your success. When trust is high, a true partnership can be developed with consultants who are willing to provide this level of relationship, as well as information and implementation.

Action. Some clients value a consultant's action-orientation and willingness to "Ready-Fire-Aim," rather than go through the usual lumbering procedures for getting things done inside the cultural or political constraints of their organization. There's a saying in the military that "Acting only after receiving more than 80 percent of the information available is procrastination."

Advice. Information is plentiful; good advice is rare. Often the value of a consultant is not the hard and fast answers he or she provides, but smart advice and options on how to proceed using the resources available.

In the modern world of business, it is useless to be a creative, original thinker unless you can also sell what you create.

—*David Ogilvy*, advertising "guru"

Myth #5: Hard work will pay off. You can work your brains out and do great things exactly as promised (and you probably have), and someone inside your organization will still be upset and unsatisfied. Why is that? Because people don't have extra-sensory perception. All the hard work in the world doesn't make a whit of difference unless your "internal" client knows what you're doing, what you've done, and what difference you're making. The truth is that *results* pay off. Strengthen your communication skills so that you can convey the exact results you want to your consultant and your senior management in a timely manner. This will generate buy-in for any project, with or without a consultant.

Don't pay for work (input), when what you really want is measurable results (output).

Myth #6: People will steal all your good ideas. One of my clients, before she actually became a client, sent me the following in an e-mail: "David, I really appreciate your willingness to give up the good stuff in our meeting today." It made me smile, because that is exactly how I get and keep clients. It's not some act or trap or manipulative trick. I'm genuinely interested in helping people inside organizations do more innovative work, generate more value, do smarter marketing, and learn to work from the heart. It's what I talk about all the time. Now, some sales-training programs call this "spilling the candy in the lobby" or "free consulting" and strongly recommend against it, on principle (and also for the consultant's financial well-being).

I disagree. I would go as far as saying that most times, you should not hire a consultant (or an employee) if they are not willing to give value first and take the risk that someone will "steal" their ideas and spec out the work to someone cheaper, or just do it themselves based on the valuable information shared. If your consultant is not open and generous with some initial information before you make a hiring decision, what makes you think he'll be open and generous afterward?

Chapter 7: Evaluating Your Consultant's Toolkit

> Don't worry about people stealing your ideas. If your ideas are any good, you'll have to ram them down people's throats.
>
> —*Howard Aiken,* electrical engineer, physicist, and computing pioneer

Myth #7: Consultants must stay focused on the issues they were brought in to solve. One of the special skills that good consultants develop over time is the ability to give their clients exactly what they need, not what they think they want.

If your organization has tried a consultant's "remedies" and they haven't worked, it's most likely because the consulting or training services were *symptom-oriented*, not *principle-oriented*.

Symptom-oriented requests sound like this:

- Our people are always complaining about our inefficient processes. We need process improvement.
- Our teams fight and argue a lot. We need some teambuilding.
- Our executives are stressed out with too much to do. We need stress management training.
- We just promoted a new crop of VPs. We need leadership development.

Symptom-oriented solutions usually don't work in the long-term, because the first problem is never the real or the only problem—there are usually underlying personal and/or organizational issues that have to be dealt with first.

Principle-oriented solutions are based in "systems thinking"—the idea that fixing one problem area in isolation without looking to the connections and impacts elsewhere is sure to cause more (and probably more severe) problems. Systems thinking embraces an expanded view of complex relationships, recurring problems (and previous attempts to fix them), and problems where the solution is not obvious or where actions may affect or be affected by the environment surrounding the issue.

Does this sound like your current situation? The key to getting the kinds of business results you need is to look beyond the typical kinds of things that you have been conditioned into wanting. A good consultant needs to be an expert diagnostician. Sometimes the issues they were initially brought in to solve emerge more clearly as mere symptoms of underlying problems that are caused elsewhere in the organization, or perhaps even outside the organization altogether. Don't let the first answer or solution that pops into your head cloud your thinking or push you into a snap decision about what kind of consulting help you need. Sometimes the most effective solutions emerge after some percolation time, which will allow the underlying issues to emerge more clearly. Collaborate with your consultant not just on the solution, but also on clearly defining the problem.

Myth #8: Change is good. Change is neither good nor bad. It is simply inevitable.

Consultants are Paid to Rock the Boat

It is vitally important that the consultants you hire be unafraid. *Require* them to rock the boat! A good consultant worth her fees will not want to hear either of the following two phrases: "We've always done it that way" and "We've never done it that way."

Part of a consultant's value lies in being able and willing to wake up clients—to force clients to pay attention to things that the consultant was, after all, called in to fix. Part of the consulting job is to be a cheerleader on steroids, and if that means getting in people's faces, including the people who sign the checks, so be it.

Chapter 7: Evaluating Your Consultant's Toolkit

Consider this scenario: A consultant gathers everyone in a conference room and makes them think about some hard issues—about their business, about their people, about their own behavior, habits, and abilities. He doesn't pull any punches, and speaks 100 percent from his expertise and his heart. People get uncomfortable. People stop talking. With arms crossed, they start to glare at him.

Does he ignore these reactions? No. He'll ask the person with the most-closed and hostile body language in the room to stand up. He'll then ask, "What do you think of this meeting so far?" The exchange goes something like this:

Client: I think you're wasting our time.

Consultant: Good. What do you think of me?

Client: [pause] I don't like you.

Consultant: You hate me. Go ahead and just say it. None of this is going to work if you don't put everything on the table, including your feelings.

Client: [slowly] All right, I hate you.

Consultant: And you hate what I'm doing to you and you don't think this project is worth your time.

Client: Yes, I hate what you're doing.

Consultant: Why is that?

As soon as the consultant asks, "Why is that?" the exchange moves to a whole new level. Now it's a conversation. Now, it's *real,* because this consultant wasn't afraid to rock the boat, pick up on emotions running high in the room, and call people on it. Psychologists call this behavior "healthy differentiation." Consultants must sometimes clearly demonstrate their separateness from the client in order to move the relationship and the results forward.

Stay Away from So-called Best Practices

> Once you think you're at the point that it's time to write it down, build the manual, and document the formula, you're no longer exploring or questioning the status quo.
>
> —*Lou Gerstner,* former chairman of IBM

The same kind of thinking expressed in the above quote is what brought IBM back from the brink of extinction. Gerstner wrote a book in 2003 titled, *Who Says Elephants Can't Dance?* in which he explained that you cannot *lead* as a consultant or as a manager by *following.* The only thing more dangerous than risking stagnation by documenting your own "success formulas" is slavishly trying to copy the success formulas of others. Yet when consultants and managers seem to be enamored by those same formulas, they are labeled "best practices."

Think about it this way: There is no practice that is better than all other possible practices if you remove it from its original context. No matter what the practice and how valuable it is in one context, it can easily be destroyed by altering things about the situation surrounding the practice. What works for others will not work for you—and certainly not in the same way. How could it? Different company, different people, different circumstances, different everything.

The fact is that successful companies blaze trails using their unique circumstances, people, leaders, and landscape—and that trail rolls up right behind them! You can't follow, and you shouldn't try. In fact, pretending that there is one "best" way has a chilling effect on our own ability to innovate. "Best practice" buzzwords become a substitute for the more difficult, less glamorous, but ultimately more powerful idea of continually innovating, tapping into your own creative resources, and continually learning, unlearning, and relearning how to get things done.

Chapter 7: Evaluating Your Consultant's Toolkit

Excellence in business simply cannot be attained by blindly copying what other organizations say that they do. A "best practice" is really just an invitation to become a pawn in someone else's game. Your job and your consultant's job is not to play like a pawn, but to win the game. You can't do that by watching someone else play.

Chapter 8
Manager as Consultant

Consultants come and go. You, as the manager, are there for the long haul. Consultants are good at various track and field events—getting things done, jumping hurdles, and vaulting themselves over bars using specialized "poles," but you are the marathon runner, operating at high performance mile after mile after mile. How do you keep it up? By developing your own set of consulting skills, tools, and attitudes. And just like athletic prowess, consulting prowess develops and grows over time if you give it focus, dedication, and practice.

This is not a book about consulting. There are thousands of books on that topic already. However, I would be remiss if I did not point out the fact that you, as an experienced manager, are in an ideal position to become an outstanding consultant yourself.

When you take on the role of internal consultant, you're being held to a higher standard. Your own experience, expertise, knowledge, and existing relationships are all part of your advanced toolkit. People will expect great things from you, especially since you're a trusted insider and have intimate knowledge of your organization and its challenges and key players, and know how to skillfully sell your ideas to the right people in the right ways at the right time.

Don't be intimidated by all these "extra" expectations—simply rise to the occasion and use good common sense. Feel free to follow the suggestions in this book for working with outside consultants. Only now, the consultant is *you!*

How to Be an Excellent Internal Consultant

An excellent internal consultant is not only a quick learner, but also a quick unlearner and relearner. Let me explain what I mean by these terms.

Learner. A learner synthesizes knowledge, information, and experience into useful advice and action.

Unlearner. An unlearner is willing to let go of old information, outdated assumptions, and lessons from past successes. What worked in the past worked in the past. Every stock prospectus has this statement: "Past performance does not guarantee future results." Unfortunately, many people simply repeat what they did before. That's like driving a car by looking in the rearview mirror.

Relearner. A relearner combines information in new ways and in specific contexts to generate innovative solutions to current business problems. Relearning is an ongoing process, not a one-time event. The more you can synthesize and enact valuable solutions, the more value you bring to your organization.

Great Ideas Needed Greatly

Great ideas are great because they are needed. Stephen Covey talks of "the urgent vs. the important." Things that are important but are not urgent do not get much attention in business. They're nice-to-have or "someday" issues. Everyone's first priority is to take care of the things that are both important *and* urgent.

Your organization will need compelling reasons to consider novel, fresh, and uncomfortable ideas. Finding a solution must be important enough to overcome our mental and physical inertia. That is why they say that necessity is the mother of invention.

Consider the following examples of great ideas needed greatly:

- The Christmas hymn *Silent Night* was written because a church organ was broken. A beautiful hymn was composed that could be sung with only a guitar for accompaniment.
- James Spangler invented the Hoover vacuum cleaner because he was afraid of losing his janitorial job once he became too old to lift the heavy carpet-cleaning machine (which also kicked up dust that made him violently sick). He needed to find another way to clean carpets.
- J. C. Hall started out importing elegantly engraved cards from Europe for Valentine's Day and Christmas. His entire inventory of cards was destroyed in a fire weeks before Valentine's Day. It was too late to get more cards from Europe. Facing financial ruin, Hall bought a small engraving firm and started designing his own Valentine cards. He then began making cards for other occasions to keep his press running year round and thus started Hallmark greeting cards.

You will be much more inventive and your organization's leaders will be much more receptive if the business need to act is great. Developing and conveying legitimate urgency around a business issue in an honest and compelling way is a skill worth developing.

> In life, you need either inspiration or desperation.
> —*Anthony Robbins*

The Art and Science of Consulting Creatively

Whether or not you will ever do any formal consulting, you can learn to think like the best consultants. The four suggestions that follow should broaden your thinking about problems and solutions.

1. Eliminate old answers. Dee Hock, the founder of VISA, said, "The problem is never how to get new ideas into your head. It's how to get the old ones out." Tolerable solutions and an "if it ain't broke, don't fix it" attitude tend to prevent us from considering better solutions. Remember, *good* ideas are the enemy of *great* ideas.

Solutions that have been kicked around for years should be temporarily off-limits in defining your problem. This seems to contradict my earlier advice to look everywhere for new ideas, but familiar solutions are not new solutions. You must ignore old answers so that you don't get misled; after all, if they were real answers, then your problem would already be solved. To free yourself to think of better alternatives, identify your current top three solutions and declare them off-limits. You can't break rules and cling to rules at the same time.

> Mere precedent is a dangerous source of authority.
> —*Andrew Jackson*

2. Attack *one* problem from *all* sides. Problem definition is a big challenge for organizations. If you held a meeting right now with the top 20 leaders inside any large organization and asked them what the organization's #1 problem is, you would more than likely get 20 different problems—10 on a good day. If you asked 100 people, you'd get 100 different problems. Nobody can solve 100 different problems at once—solutions will never emerge.

You must work hard to clearly define the problem. Too often, there is little or no agreement on what the key problems are. Everyone assumes they know, and everyone's assumptions are different. If you can articulate a single specific, well-defined problem, you will be able to work toward a single specific, well-defined solution with focus and energy. If there are multiple problems, attack them one at a time.

Make your problem definitions clear to everyone. You never know where a breakthrough idea will come from. For example, if your problem is how to grow revenue by 15 percent annually, then "15 Percent Annual Revenue Growth" should be posted in every office, or have buttons made up that say "How do we sell 15% more?" Divisional and departmental objectives should be linked to this key objective: The company's customer service group can define its objective as "Reduce service call hold time to two minutes to support growing revenue by 15 percent," and the Western division can define its objective as "Increase quarterly sales to $16 million to support 15 percent revenue growth." Both objectives link to the key objective.

If *my* problem and *your* problem and *our* problem are the same, then everything we do will result in a concentrated, singular effort to solve it from all sides.

> A problem clearly stated is a problem half solved.
> —*Dorothea Brande*

3. A sketch sells better than a painting. Anytime you come up with a breakthrough idea, you will be tempted to create a lengthy memo detailing the idea, or even worse, create a 50-slide PowerPoint presentation laying out all the brilliant aspects and benefits of your freshly invented plan.

This would be a mistake. Your stakeholders will probably end up doing one of two things: Reject the plan, or resent it.

Never deal in highly polished or "finished" products early in the process. If you parade in your finished product, there is nothing for your client to do. It's not his work, it's your work. The client doesn't feel involved, committed, or even included. What's more, the client won't see the big ideas behind your detailed solution.

Instead, show your internal client a sketch of the plan. Explain it—tell the story behind it to enhance its meaning and relevance. Engage your client's imagination. Get the client involved. Collaborate. Co-create. When you leave the solution somewhat open, there's room for customization, adaptation, interpretation, and lots of client input.

Consultants help clients fulfill their dreams for their organizations. People like to be engaged and involved in their own dreams. You can't dream for them.

4. Get lost. Why are things always in the last place we look for them? Because we stop looking once we find them! For keys, that makes sense. For business answers, it can be debilitating. Abraham Lincoln once said, "Towering genius disdains a beaten path. It seeks regions hitherto unexplored." The problem with experts is that they have done a lot of exploring and have beaten down a lot of paths. In fact, some experts are convinced that they have the complete map; why keep searching when a perfectly viable path is right in front of us?

But if you never get lost and have to find new paths, you stop progress and you stop innovation. Your old answers start to limit your current options. Don't let experts or complacent naysayers undermine your capacity for innovation.

The Power of Encouragement

A group of frogs were traveling together through the woods when two of them fell into a deep pit. All the other frogs gathered around the pit. When they saw how deep the pit was, they told the two frogs that they were as good as dead.

The two frogs ignored the comments and tried to jump up out of the pit with all of their might. The other frogs kept telling them to stop—that they were as good as dead.

Finally, one of the frogs took heed to what the other frogs were saying and gave up. He fell down and died. The other frog continued to jump as hard as he could. Once again, the crowd of frogs yelled at him to stop the pain and just die. He jumped even harder, and finally made it out.

When he got out, the other frogs said, "Did you not hear us?" The frog explained to them that he was deaf. He thought they were encouraging him the entire time.

This story teaches two lessons:

1. The power of life and death is in the tongue. An encouraging word to someone who is down can lift them up and help them make it through the day.

2. A destructive word to someone who is down might just kill them. Be careful what you say: Speak life to those who cross your path.

It's sometimes hard to believe that an encouraging word can go such a long way. It's far too easy to speak words that can rob someone of their spirit in difficult times. Special is the individual who will take the time to encourage others.

> My ability to arouse enthusiasm among people is the greatest asset I possess. The way to develop the best that is in a person is by appreciation and encouragement.
>
> —*Charles Schwab*

The Secret Sauce: Intellect Plus Intuition

According to Phil Hodgson, author of *What Do High Performance Managers Really Do?* leaders who use their intuition effectively and continuously are likely to have a number of common characteristics. Here are some of the most important.

> **Leaders Who Use Their Intuition . . .**
>
> - Make decisions quickly and confidently. They are willing to back their judgment, and don't spend large amounts of time agonizing over options.
> - Use data only when necessary. The huge multi-dimensional data analysis with charts and graphs and projections is a peripheral tool, if used at all.
> - Recognize the importance of their own intuitive skill, and continue to pay attention to developing it through use.
> - Accept and encourage ideas, whatever their source or apparent usefulness, at every stage.
> - Act on intuitive judgments, rather than question them.
> - Accept no rigid or wrong method of doing things. If something feels, looks, or seems right, they will do it.

Here are what four leaders who use their intuition say about it:

> Lou Gerstner: "Once I have a feeling for the choices, I have no problems with the decisions."
>
> Sir David Simon, former Chairman of British Petroleum: "You don't have to discuss things. You can sense it. The tingle is as important as the intellect."
>
> Jack Welch: "Here at the head office, we don't go very deep into much of anything, but we have a smell of everything. Smell, feel, touch, listen, then allocate. Make bets, with people and dollars. And make mistakes."
>
> John Naisbitt: "Intuition becomes increasingly valuable in the new information society, precisely because there is so much data."

Consultants and Managers Blazing the Trail Together

Now that you're familiar with what to look for, what to ask for, and what to watch for when working with consultants, you are ideally equipped to work shoulder-to-shoulder with consultants in the pursuit of organizational excellence.

Author Terry Orlick writes that the experiences of exceptional performers in all fields (sports, the sciences, the arts, law, medicine, business, and academics) suggest that there are seven elements critical to excellence: commitment, belief, full focus, positive images, mental readiness, distraction control, and constructive evaluation.

**Managers and Consultants:
Elements Critical to Excellence**

You can examine how closely you come to the ideal in each area by asking yourself the following questions. Thinking about your own responses will make you a better manager *and* consultant. Refer to them whenever you take on a project alone or with a team.

Commitment
- Are your goals clear, challenging, and targeted toward being your best?
- Do you work at improving something every day, in every "performance"?
- Is your commitment to training, practice, or preparation strong enough to take you to your high-level goals?
- Is your commitment to respect your personal needs for rest, balance, recovery, and good nutrition strong enough to take you to your goals?

Belief/Self-Confidence
- Do you believe in your capacity to reach your goal(s)?
- Are you putting yourself in situations that give you the greatest chance of believing in yourself and achieving your goals?
- Do you think and act in ways that make you feel positive and confident?
- Do you have a plan to get there?
- Do you trust your plan and your preparation?
- Will you free yourself to let good things unfold?

(continued)

Managers and Consultants:
Elements Critical to Excellence *(concluded)*

Full Focus
- Do you know what focus works best for you?
- Do you have a plan to consistently get into your best focus?
- Do you work at improving your focus? How?
- Do you focus on doing the little things that work best for you every day, for the duration of your performance?

Positive Images
- Do you imagine yourself performing (or interacting) the way you would ideally like to?
- Do you imagine yourself achieving your goals?
- Do you imagine yourself doing the little things that will allow you to achieve your larger goals?
- Do you "wake up" your positive images by acting in ways that will take you a step closer to your goals each day?

Mental Readiness
- Do you carry a perspective that centers on ongoing learning and growing?
- Do you mentally prepare yourself to live and perform your best? Consistently?
- Do you trust yourself to free your performance to unfold?
- Do you remain open to the creativity of the moment and the dynamics of the situation?

Distraction Control
- Do you carry a perspective or focus that allows you to avoid, minimize, or take control of distractions?
- Do you maintain your best focus even when faced with setbacks or distractions?
- Do you prepare yourself to deal with errors or setbacks as they arise, and focus on quickly regaining control?

Constructive Evaluation
- Do you draw lessons out of every experience or every performance? (*What went well? What needs work?*)
- Do you act on those lessons every day or at every opportunity?
- Do you reflect on the role that your "mindset" played in your performance?
- Do you act on those reflections?

Chapter 8: Manager as Consultant

> If you want to achieve excellence, you can get there today. As of this second, quit doing less-than-excellent work.
>
> —*Thomas J. Watson,* founder of IBM

Great managers and great consultants are trailblazers and leaders. A trailblazing leader:

- Sets direction
- Mobilizes individual commitment
- Engenders organizational capability
- Demonstrates personal character

Let's take a closer look at each trailblazing characteristic:

A trailblazing leader sets direction. He or she analyzes the field for trends; understands external events; focuses on the future; articulates tangible vision, values, and strategy; inspires a shared purpose; and creates a climate for success.

A trailblazing leader mobilizes individual commitment. He or she builds collaborative relationships; promotes cooperative goals and builds trust; shares power and authority; listens more than tells; elicits participation; exerts power through dignity and respect for others; uses a variety of approaches to get the best out of everyone; creates opportunities for people to contribute their strongest and highest personal talents to the team effort; manages attention with powerful stories; and uses language that touches the heart.

A trailblazing leader engenders organizational capability. He or she integrates and orchestrates activities of various groups; vigorously challenges the status quo; experiments and takes risks; seeks simpler methods to achieve better results; and uses the inputs and stimuli of others to catalyze change.

A trailblazing leader demonstrates personal character. He or she practices what is preached; leads by example; maintains a positive self-image; balances self-confidence with humility; continually sharpens his or her insight into the realities of the world and into group members; seeks broad opportunities to learn; learns from mistakes; remains open to criticism; deals effectively with complex, ambiguous, and contradictory situations; possesses personal charm and a sense of humor; thinks through problems in fresh ways; and tries new and sometimes counter-intuitive alternatives.

The Next Chapter is Up to You

We've covered a lot of ground. By now you understand who consultants are, what they really do, when you need them, why you need them, and how you can make the most of your day-to-day relationship while you develop your own skills as a manager, a leader, and a consultant in your own right.

I hope that *The Manager's Pocket Guide to Using Consultants* sheds some light on the art and science of "clienting" smart. I'm tempted to title my next book *The Consultant's Pocket Guide to Managers,* but then I remember how many books about management have already been written!

If you're willing to accept nothing less than excellence from yourself and from others, you will greatly increase the chances of implementing excellent, innovative, and collaborative solutions—not just now, but also into the future, as you work with challenges that have yet to emerge.

Best of luck on the journey!

About the Author

David Newman is a marketing and innovation consultant and professional speaker with more than 15 years of experience working with Fortune 500 clients. He is an active member of the National Speakers Association, speaking regularly on his four areas of expertise: marketing, sales, innovation, and intrapreneurship, and has written several books on business topics. His writing has also appeared in *Business Digest, Sales & Marketing Management, Selling Power, Entrepreneur,* and *Business2Business* magazine (where he is a regular columnist).

He is the founder of UNCONSULTING, a firm featured in *Bull Market: Companies That Can Help You Make Something Happen,* by Seth Godin (2004).

David was selected by the Stanford Graduate School of Business as one of twenty consultants certified to teach Stanford's *Creativity in Business* MBA curriculum to corporations. He is also certified by the Center for Organizational Design and is a Get Clients Now licensed facilitator.

During his in-house training and development career, David won several awards for his work in developing global live training and e-learning curricula and integrating firm-wide learning programs into corporate university formats.

He lives with his wife, Vanessa Christman, and their children Rebecca and Charlie in Bryn Mawr, Pennsylvania. He can be contacted at the following address:

> David Newman
> UNCONSULTING
> 121 Rodney Circle
> Bryn Mawr, PA 19010
> (610) 527-5325
> www.unconsulting.com
> david@unconsulting.com

www.ingramcontent.com/pod-product-compliance
Lightning Source LLC
Chambersburg PA
CBHW071730090426
42738CB00011B/2448